D1569826

"My Brother Esau
Is a Hairy Man"

"My Brother Esau Is a Hairy Man"

Hair and Identity in Ancient Israel

SUSAN NIDITCH

OXFORD
UNIVERSITY PRESS

2008

OXFORD
UNIVERSITY PRESS

Oxford University Press, Inc., publishes works that further
Oxford University's objective of excellence
in research, scholarship, and education.

Oxford New York
Auckland Cape Town Dar es Salaam Hong Kong Karachi
Kuala Lumpur Madrid Melbourne Mexico City Nairobi
New Delhi Shanghai Taipei Toronto

With offices in
Argentina Austria Brazil Chile Czech Republic France Greece
Guatemala Hungary Italy Japan Poland Portugal Singapore
South Korea Switzerland Thailand Turkey Ukraine Vietnam

Published by Oxford University Press, Inc.
198 Madison Avenue, New York, New York 10016

www.oup.com

Oxford is a registered trademark of Oxford University Press

Library of Congress Cataloging-in-Publication Data
Niditch, Susan.
My brother Esau is a hairy man : hair and identity
in ancient Israel / Susan Niditch.
    p. cm.
Includes bibliographical references.
ISBN 978-0-19-518114-2
1. Hair—Religious aspects—Judaism.
2. Hair—Social aspects. I. Title.
BM729.H34N53 2008
221.8'3915—dc22   2007026347

9 8 7 6 5 4 3 2 1

Printed in the United States of America
on acid-free paper

Acknowledgments

I thank the National Endowment for the Humanities, which generously supported this project with a Fellowship for College Teachers in 2005–2006. I would also like to thank the trustees of Amherst College, who provided sabbatical leave and a grant from the Axel Schupf Fund for Intellectual Life to travel to the British Museum to study relevant pieces in the Assyrian collection. In London, Dr. Dominique Collon provided excellent guidance, for which I thank her. I benefitted from the assistance and encouragement of a number of additional colleagues: Dan Ben-Amos, Elizabeth Bloch-Smith, Cynthia R. Chapman, John J. Collins, Edward L. Greenstein, JoAnn Hackett, Yehudit Heller, Peter Machinist, Carol Meyers, Margaret A. Mills, J. J. Roberts, John M. Russell, Leong Seow, Lawrence E. Stager, Robert R. Wilson, Irene J. Winter, and members of the Colloquium for Biblical Research, where I first presented a paper on hair in the Hebrew Bible. As always, my dear husband Robert Doran discussed my work with me along the way, providing thoughtful suggestions and enthusiastic encouragement. My daughter Rebecca carefully proofread an early draft of the manuscript and provided her own creative and sensitive insights. I thank her and my daughter Elizabeth, who in recent years has introduced me to a number of works in sociology and women's studies that have influenced this book in various ways. I also want to mention my students, particularly those in a course on "The Body and Ancient Judaism," in which I began to explore in depth topics relating to the body, religion, and Israelite culture.

Contents

"My Brother Esau
Is a Hairy Man"

1

Introduction

In the fall of 2003, the Boston Red Sox had little hope of advancing to the World Series. They were about to face the Oakland A's at Fenway Park in a night game that could have ended the season for the talented but beleaguered team. The Red Sox had not won the World Series since 1917, and even their fans were convinced that they labored under "the curse of the Bambino," Babe Ruth, a former Red Sox hero, traded to the Yankees in 1920. In an effort to change their luck, a number of the players shaved their heads.

"About 15 of us shaved our heads," said Millar (Red Sox first baseman). We've lost four in a row. This quirky thing sometimes works and we'll see what happens" (*Boston Globe*, 2003, A-1).

In the summer of 2004, a graduate student took intensive Chinese language training, studying in Beijing. She continued to follow her early morning exercise routine, a five-mile run. She had beautiful, long, curly, chestnut brown hair, and it flew behind her as she sped along the busy streets of the Chinese capital. The old women of the city rose early also. As she passed, one said, "Look at her hair. It is so ugly!" Others turned aside in fear or disapproval. She understood both the Chinese words and the body language.

Artist Anne Wilson weaves, shapes, dyes, and frames human hair to make thought-provoking sculptures about human identity, aesthetics, physicality, mortality, and gender. In the 1998 piece *Lost*, exhibited in various museums of art and currently held in a private collection, the artist created an eerie, mood-altering cameo: a cascade of white

3

linen material, evoking a curtain or other gathered, fulsome length of cloth, embroidered with dark human hair and draped over a simple white chair of the sort one might find in a country kitchen (fig. 1).

Wilson writes, "The piece is made by hand stitching human hair onto a white damask table linen. There are a couple hundred hand bound button holes through which a black leather cord is laced.... In these sculptures I use methods and materials that are familiar, intimate, quite delicate, and culturally loaded. The visceral nature of human hair is in contrast to the formality of white linen, and sets up an aesthetic of oppositional tendencies" (e-mail to the author, October 2, 2005). From a distance the pattern is a dense, black blur at the bend where it lies over the back of the chair; gradually a weblike, grayer, and lighter design emerges closer to the floor.

Art critic Christine Temin describes the piece as "a shroudlike garment" and interprets, "the body that might once have inhabited it is truly lost, leaving only the black hair behind, sewn onto the cloth" (*Boston Globe*, 2002, N8). The artist writes, "*Lost* is about the loss of the physical body; about mortality.

FIGURE 1. *Lost* by Anne Wilson. Photograph courtesy of Lester Marx.

The displaced hair is lost, separated from the body, graduated over a large cloth that may reference something like a garment or curtain, gathered and draped over a chair" (e-mail to the author, October 2, 2005). The label from the exhibition at the Chicago Museum of Contemporary Art (July 8–October 1, 200) describes, "A leather cord is pulled through hand stitched belt loops, gathering this monumental cloth so that the form it takes is far removed from its original use as a table cloth. The presence it now assumes is more bodily than domestic. Wilson stitched the hair thickly in the central section of the cloth, thinning it out at the edges, reflecting the organic reality of how hair grows unevenly on the body." Wilson's sculpture evokes a variety of responses and nuances of interpretation, as she and others try to express what woven, detached hair says about loss.

Hair plays an integral and intricate role in the way human beings represent themselves. It is related to natural and cultural identity, to personal and group anxieties, and to private and public aspirations, aesthetics, and passages. In this book I explore culture and identity in ancient Israel as expressed, shaped, and reinforced in images of hair, a complex symbol drawn from the body. Hair can be severed without pain; it is curiously part of and separate from the body—hair itself is not alive, and yet it grows. Its appearance may transform the person or disguise her, create or alter identity (see Levine 1995, 85–86). Shaved, clipped or long and loose, wildly free or carefully shaped, tied, or tamed, hair may be a sign of youth or age, womanly charm or manly vigor, an indicator of uncleanness or madness, of one's place in society or one's removal from the social realm, and this list only begins to suggest the possibilities of meaning.

Two excellent articles have been written on biblical hair, one by Saul Olyan (1998), who examines shaving rites as means of ritual transformation, and one by Gregory Mobley (1997), who explores a host of ancient Near Eastern hairy men who take their place on the border of nature and culture. I return to the work of these scholars in due course, but the time has come to place the study of biblical hair in a wider and deeper methodological framework concerning symbols, the body, culture, and hair.

Over the last decade, there has been an explosion of scholarly interest in the relationship between culture and the body. Particularly influential have been Foucault's (1980) and Bourdieu's (1984) studies of the complex ways in which culture is "inscribed" on the body. Susan Bordo (1999; 1993) examines the influences of mass culture upon men's and women's views of their bodies and their identities, both sexual and social. With her study of women's relationships to food as described in medieval sources, Carolyn Bynum (1987) challenges conventional notions about the supposed dichotomy between spirit and flesh in Christian asceticism, while Elizabeth Grosz (1994) challenges as too simplistic the contrast frequently drawn between nature and culture in attempts to explain imagery pertaining to the body. Gananath Obeyesekere (1981) points to the rigid distinctions sometimes drawn between "public and private symbols," between "culture and emotion" (46), and discusses the ways in which hair and other motifs are symbolically rooted in shared human imagery, taking on personal and social meaning depending on the individual's experience and his or her cultural context.

Moira Gatens (1996) writes of an "imaginary body," exploring the roles played by socialization and individual subjectivity in constructing ideas of male and female. For Gatens, the imaginary body is also the "situated body"— situated, that is, in history and culture (see the excellent review and analysis by Amy Hollywood [1999]). One special issue of the *Journal of American Folklore*, devoted to "bodylore" (Young and Babcock 1994), treats the body as discourse, examining the body as a means of communication, while another issue, on construing the European social body (Bendix and Noyes 1998), discusses the relationship between costume and culture and the relationships among clothing, politics, and identity. Scholars of religion have also produced a wide range of studies focusing on the body within various traditions (see Coakley [1997], Law [1995], Arthur [1999], Becher [1991], Boyarin [1993], Eilberg-Schwartz [1992], and Eilberg-Schwartz and Doniger [1995]).

One of the excellent methodological features shared by these seminal works and others related to them in various theoretical trajectories is the appreciation for complexity and complication. Those studies that resist settling for simple dichotomies or one-to-one correspondences between hairstyle and meaning will serve as the best guides and suggest the most useful, rich, and thought-provoking questions in exploring the meanings and messages of biblical hair. Three interesting models emerge from recurring theoretical concerns in such studies of the body, religion, culture, and hair and offer a good range of approaches to the study of hair in ancient Israel.

The First Model: Individual Body, Social Body, and Body Politic

The first model is provided by medical anthropologists Nancy Scheper-Hughes and Margaret Lock (1987) and applied to the study of hair by Barbara Miller (1998). Scheper-Hughes and Lock suggest exploring the meanings of "body" in terms of three interrelated categories. First is the "individual body," the "phenomenological sense of the lived experience of the body-self" (1987, 7). One might ask how a person's hair makes him or her feel, what hair means to people in their personal lives, how hair represents them or serves as an extension of self, a critical source of their own embodiment. As Obeyesekere (1981) learned in interviewing women mystics in Sri Lanka who wear their hair in long, matted ropes, the hair is personal and has to do with that person's life experience, her anxieties, psychology, and idiosyncrasies. She loves her hair and has an emotional attachment to it (7, 37, 40). In her study *Hair Matters,* Ingrid Banks (2000) interviewed a wide range of African-American women concerning their hair and received a number of responses drawn from the women's experience of self. Altering or relaxing their hair or wearing it in a natural style may make them feel empowered (63), and their hair has a good deal to do with self-image. We might ask the questions concerning the self and hair in relation to the biblical portrayal of Absalom. The prince wears long, thick tresses, cutting them once a year and determining how much the beautiful locks weigh. Why does the biblical writer imagine such a man as headed for a fall? What does it say about the sense of self with which the biblical author endows Absalom, the would-be usurper of his father's throne?

Banks (2000) also explores the ways in which hairstyles and treatments of hair are integrally related to social and cultural identity (22, 42), a theme likewise found in the study by Nowile Rooks (1996), another scholar who studies the significance of hair in African-American cultures (4, 20). Similarly, Obeyesekere (1981) emphasizes the complex ways in which the personal intertwines with the public and the cultural. Social context is critical; were there not certain assumptions and expectations concerning hairstyle in Sri Lanka, where the mystic has lived and developed, her personal response to her own hair might differ considerably. Similarly, Jeannette Marie Mageo (1994) writes of the Samoan woman's hair as part of her "symbolic body" or "imaginary body" (see also Gatens 1996). The hair holds personal meaning to the woman and is involved in a variety of fantasies, identities, symbolizations, and projections, but even these are rooted in cultural context, in a "grammar of hair" as Olivelle (1998, 11–12) puts it, in the woman's cultural expectations and the conventions of her social world. Thus a second category offered by Scheper-Hughes and Lock is "the social body."

Influenced by the work of anthropologist Mary Douglas (1966), Scheper-Hughes and Lock explore the ways in which body serves as a natural symbol. Like Bordo (1993) and Bourdieu (1984), Douglas asks how the social and cultural is inscribed on the body. Similarly, Raymond Firth (1973) argues that hair allows humans to use "their own physical raw material in terms of the social norms to provide indices to their personality and make statements about their conception of their role, their social position and changes in these" (298). Thus Julia Thompson (1998) writes of women's hair in Nepal, "the symbolic message hair sends to others can…be indicative of a specific cultural state or status (nun, widow, renouncer, vow keeper); or indicative of particular life circumstances (caste, class, nationality). Moreover it might be different now than ten years ago or perhaps ten years hence" (250). James Watson (1998) asks what the destitute young men in colonial Hong Kong of the 1960s were saying about their personal condition and social status by wearing long, unkempt hair. He asks about the "social management of hair" (179) and explores how this modern phenomenon may relate to a lengthy Chinese tradition concerning the demeanor of ghosts, bandits, and rebels. What message is Absalom sending in wearing his hair long? What cultural signals has he absorbed concerning manhood or leadership or prowess in war that are expressed and reinforced by his long hair?

The third category offered by Scheper-Hughes and Lock (1987) is really a subset of the social body, "the body politic." "The body politic" interweaves with "the individual body" as well. This level of meaning, grounded in the work of Michel Foucault, deals with "the regulation, surveillance, and control of bodies" (7). Hair thus expresses and shapes specific messages about power or subversion of that power. As Mageo (1994) notes, an issue to consider is whether the hairstyle is worn voluntarily (424). Influenced by the suggestion of C. D. Hallpike (1969) that "cutting hair equals social control" (263), Weikun Cheng (1998) shows how enforced wearing of the queue in Qing China "reflected the Manchus drive to submit Hans to the minority's political and cultural hegemonies and its symbolic standardization of the people's political ideology" (128). In the biblical tradition, the woman taken captive by Israelites in Deuteronomy 21 whose hair is shaved is clearly in the grip of someone's else's power. She has been made to represent the control of her enemies, her transformation by her captors, and her removal from her own society and cultural environment.

Scheper-Hughes and Lock's (1987) concept of "the domestication of the individual body" (126) leads to questions about the ways in which members of a social group are expected to wear the dominant hairstyle that expresses their gender, economic status, or other form of identity. In a similar vein, both Banks (1996) and Rooks (2000) explore what a white society has told African-American women about the acceptability or beauty of their hair. They also examine the ways in which their own families may educate young women about such matters. The Afro hairdo made a genuine political statement in the 1960s about African-American identity, the politics of change, and the demand for acceptance on one's own terms. Julia Thompson (1998) describes a woman in Kathmandu who shaves her head in mourning for her mother, thereby engaging in the ritual behavior of men. She is thus "positioned to reject, rework, and reconceptualize (her) identities and their associated meanings" (237). What sort of statement would have been made by the voluntary female Nazir who took it upon herself to follow the instructions outlined Numbers 6 not to cut her hair for a specified period of time?

A Second Model: Victor Turner's Symbolic Analysis

Many of the scholars who provide us with excellent models, including Watson (1998), Olivelle (1998), Obeyesekere (1981), Mageo (1994), and Hershman (1974), emphasize that cultural context and personal framework are critical in understanding the meanings and messages of hair (see also Uberoi (1967, 88–90; Olyan 1998, 621–22). Short hair does not always mean social control (Hallpike 1969), nor does long hair always mean freedom. Hair is not necessarily a symbol of the genitals or of sexuality in all cultures or settings (see Berg 1951, and the critique by Leach 1967). Hair, moreover, can mean many things simultaneously and can operate on various levels, as Scheper-Hughes and Lock's (1987) analytical categories indicate.

Another important model is provided by Victor Turner (1967) who sought to understand how an outsider might discover the meanings of symbols within cultures. His methodology was an important influence on studies of hair by Alf Hiltebeitel (1998b) and Patrick Olivelle (1998). Turner refers to three levels of examination, the "exegetical," the "operational," and the "positional." At the exegetical level, one seeks to ascertain what people within the culture think about the symbol. Scholars such as Obeyesekere and Olivelle are able to interview living people and ask them about their views of their hair. Of course, as Uberoi (1967) notes, plumbing the meanings of essential cultural or sacred symbols is no easy task: "it is a process like that of ascertaining the grammar and syntax of a language which cannot be done by simple inquiry from a native speaker or informant" (89). Or as Hiltebeitel (1998b) writes, "we must distinguish between what people say about festivals they participate in themselves, and what we draw from wider associations" (146). The same applies to the examination of the meanings of hair. Nevertheless, those of us who work with ancient texts, without access to living participants in the culture, envy our colleagues who have access to such living resources.

Hiltebeitel (1998b) also made use of classical sources, Sanskrit and Tamil texts, to delve into the meaning of women's hairstyles in classical Indian tradition. In a similar way, we have access to the traditional texts of the Hebrew Bible, which mention hair in a variety of ritual and narrative contexts, to an array of archaeological remains that provide evidence of material culture, and to the images of ancient Near Eastern art. All such sources must be handled with care, however. Issues of authorship, provenance, dating, and relevance come to the fore as do knotty questions concerning the relationship of ancient Israelites and their varied cultures to the multivoiced, many layered, often ideologically oriented texts of the Hebrew Bible. One will have to ask whose views are presented, who shaped particular descriptions and for what purpose, how typical or widespread such views of the meaning of hair may have been, and how the slow evolution of the biblical tradition may relate to evolving views of hair as a manifestation of the individual body, the social body, or the body politic. The same caution applies to Turner's "operational level."

Turner (1967) suggests that we explore the operation of the symbol in specific contexts. What do ancient Israelites appear to do with hair in ritual settings such as those related to the assumption and completion of the Nazirite vow, described in Numbers 6? Men and women who take on this vow grow their hair; at certain points, they cut the hair, burn the hair, and so on. How does meaning emerge in such acts? Again, in dealing with biblical descriptions, one must ask who preserved this material, why, and when. Answers are not easy. Where, moreover, does such a description fit in the larger corpus of the Hebrew Bible and the larger context of other descriptions of Israelite ritual and symbolic content? Do such descriptions relate, if at all, to nonbiblical evidence about hair in ancient Israel or in the larger ancient Near Eastern context? This brings us to Turner's "positional level."

As Olivelle (1998, 12) puts the question, what is the symbolic grammar within which such practices are located? How does hair as revealed in biblical texts seem to relate to other symbols of the body in Israelite culture? Do these various symbols combine to make comments on age, gender, sacredness, and ethnicity, drawing lines between child and adult, male and female, holy and mundane, us and them?

A Third Model: Obeyesekere and the Genesis of Symbols

In addition to frameworks offered by Scheper-Hughes and Lock (1987) and Turner (1967) is a third model, offered by Obeyesekere (1981). In his study of the relationship between the private and the public in symbolic usage, Obeyesekere is particularly interested in the origins, development, and variations on key defining symbols such as hair. Summarizing the work of Olivelle (1998), Obeyesekere (1998) notes that hair has "a root meaning and on this root meaning (or rather a set of root meanings) a culture can erect its own 'grammar' or semiotics of hair.... The root symbolism of hair is not static and it can get all sorts of accretions" (xii).

All humans, Obeyesekere (1981) suggests in a Jungian vein, may share certain symbols that "emerge from the wellsprings of our unconscious and then, mediated through culture, [are] transformed by our conscious rational and cognitive faculties" (9). Obeyesekere is interested in the "link between symbol formation and personal experience, and the psychological significance of the symbol.... The psychological meaning of the symbol is in turn embodied in the dominant myths of Hindu culture" (1981, 40). Thus, for him, there is a feedback loop between deep-seated symbols of the unconscious, cultural context, personal experience, and the human being's creative capacity for inventiveness. Obeyesekere's insights are applicable to the Israelite case. In approaching biblical literature and nonbiblical evidence of ancient Israelite attitudes toward hair, we need to think about universals and specific cultural contexts and consider the intentions of individual composers and artists who create narrative scenes involving hair in verbal and nonverbal media or who describe certain ritual actions.

Models for Dealing with Nonverbal Material

John Berger (1977) has written that "every image embodies a way of seeing" (10). Although Berger's focus ranges from the oil paintings of the Renaissance to modern advertising, his observations and questions are also relevant to ancient art and representations of hair embodied in those images. Berger's suggestions are relevant as well to biblical texts relating to hair and resonate with methodological approaches found in this book.

Berger reminds the viewer to be aware of the cultural expectations, influences, and conventions behind artistic images. He asks, for example, in exploring a portrait by seventeenth-century Dutch painter Franz Hals, if the average Dutchman of this period regularly wore his hat tipped to the side and, if so, what sort of message he meant to convey (15). Is the painting's male subject with the odd expression paralyzed or inebriated and, if the latter, was this acceptable or unacceptable in society? Is there a cultural statement in the painting, a political and subversive one created by the starving artist? Berger asks why particular paintings were created and what or whose interests they were intended to serve. Where was a painting displayed, in a public space or in a private, family space? He asks, moreover, how we as lovers of art or scholarly experts find and determine meaning in representational art. What do we bring to the work from our own experience and training, culturally or personally? How does moving an ancient relief from its original setting in tomb to the gallery of a European museum alter and affect the impression it conveys and our understanding of it? How is it affected when viewed in a reproduction or in a photograph?

Berger thus presents us with a host of questions concerning culture, convention, setting, and interpretation, questions to keep in mind in exploring Egyptian reliefs that reveal Philistine hairstyles or Assyrian portrayals of conquered Judeans who are depicted with particular hairstyles. How would these representations have looked in their original settings? Who would have commissioned them and created them, and for what purpose? How do debates among scholars and our modern field of study affect what we see in these ancient images of hair?

Nonverbal material thus presents special challenges. The excellent essays in *Hair in African Culture* (Sieber and Herreman 2000), a work produced in connection with a major exhibition held at the Museum for African Art in New York from February 9 to May 2000, provide models that help assess art and evidence of material culture relating to the multilayered meanings of hair in ancient Israel. In an introductory essay, Roy Sieber (2000a, 15) underscores the ways in which hair "can serve to identify ethnic origin, gender, phase of life, status, as well as personal taste," themes discussed above. Sieber, however, also emphasizes that actual hairstyles and artistic representations of hair have "a major aesthetic component" (15). A similar set of emphases is found in the study by Niangi Batulukisi (2000). Hairstyle has to do with discourse, is "an element of social communication," and identifies the wearer, but also reflects the "human desire to modify nature, to create. Hairstyling, then, is truly an artistic discipline" (25, 26).

The essays in *Hair and African Culture* also raise important methodological issues about the relationship between "depictions of coiffure and the real world" (Sieber 2000a, 15). Frank Herreman (2000) asks, "Does the artist copy from nature or not?" (54). This is an extremely important question as we explore hair in ancient Near Eastern art and in the creative inventions of the Hebrew Bible. Herreman answers his question by addressing context and culture. One has to know the conventions of particular cultures and whether or not precise copying of real life would be considered positive or negative from an aesthetic perspective. In the material he studies, for example, "sculptors are more inspired by what they know than by what they see. The artist does not hesitate to accentuate what is considered important in his culture" (54). Similarly, Babatunde Lawal (2000) suggests that Yoruba masks and figure sculptures can be used to "illustrate the major styles, though they are often idealized in art for aesthetic purposes" (96). Concerning Israelite hair, Elizabeth Bloch-Smith asks in a similar vein, "Is what is depicted a true representation of hairstyle or rather a stylized rendition" (e-mail to the author, June 25, 2005)? In contrast, William Siegman's (2000) study of women's hair and masks in Southern Sierra Leone and Western Liberia suggests that it may be possible "to trace a history of hairstyle fashion through the representation of coiffure on sowei masks" (74) Here, "the representation of hairstyles on sculpture...is among the most detailed and realistic in any style region in Africa" (77).

Recurring themes in the studies of hair in African art concern variation between regions and villages and the representations of hairstyles of those considered to be foreigners. Few examples of pictorial or sculptural art depicting human beings have been found among the material remains of ancient Israelite cultures, an issue that should be addressed briefly at the outset.

It is axiomatic that ancient Israelites eschewed pictorial representations of the body, of people and daily life, for supposed theological reasons, namely an implicit association between such imagery and idolatry. It is suggested that figures might be worshipped as deities or considered to be representations of foreign gods in a world in which only Yhwh counted as true God, or that they might be taken as demeaning, humanlike representations of the ineffable, transcendent deity himself. Such suggestions, common in the conventional wisdom rather than among biblical scholars, greatly oversimplify the complex religions of ancient Israel and the beliefs of various sorts of Yahwists. In fact, both Yhwh and other competing deities are anthropomorphized in various ways in the written artifacts of ancient Israelite religion. The Bible also testifies to a lively theological disagreement between Israelites who were aniconic and those who allowed for iconic representations of the deity (see, for example, Judges 8 concerning Gideon's "ephod," an iconic statuary employed in some sort of Yahwistic ritual setting, and also Judges 17). It is the aniconic wing that is represented in the second commandment of Exodus 22:4, "You will not make for yourself any graven image." Others allowed for conceiving of the power of the deity as invested in various sorts of icons or perhaps disassociated representations of the deity from other sorts of representations. As noted by Narkiss (1985, 9), "it is certain that this injunction was never interpreted as an absolute prohibition against every figurative representation." Most of this material has been lost, and only hints remain of representational art, a few examples of which may pertain to our study of hair, such as the headpieces of the difficult-to-interpret graffiti figures from Kuntillet 'Ajrud and the hairstyles of the many small female figurines unearthed by archaeologists that may have functioned in some sort of household religion. Admittedly, we have few examples of Israelites representing hairstyles in art, and instead have to rely on portrayals of Israelite hair by artists of other cultures.

Neighboring cultures of Egypt and Assyria have left rich representational corpora in various media. Among these works are some representations of Israelites or, more often, of Syrians. Many questions arise. Can we be sure that those represented are Israelites and, even if so, did Egyptians, for example, properly represent Israelites' hair or see it as the Israelites did? Elizabeth Bloch-Smith asks of representations of Israelites, "Does the hairstyle imitate a foreign cosmopolitan custom" (e-mail to the author, June 25, 2005)? Are Israelites being portrayed as Syrians by the artisans of a conquering power? Can we assume that Israelites wore their hair in the fashion favored by neighboring Syrians, many more of whom are represented in ancient Near Eastern art? As Sieber (2000a) notes, in Africa there are differences in hairstyle "that exist between closely related groups living at no great geographical distance from each other" (16). Similarly, Vaughan (2000) notes that "hairstyle can reflect cultural identity even in a small geographic area" (111). While artistic representations of hairstyles in the ancient Near East are valuable resources in exploring hair in ancient Israel, they must be approached with caution, and they raise as many questions as they provide answers.

Ancient Israel: Environment, Natural and Political

The approaches offered and the complex questions evoked by these various studies of hair in non-Israelite environments all have something to do with context. Hair takes on meaning within cultural settings and within the framework of individual experience. To contextualize hair in ancient Israel, we need to explore who the Israelites were, where they lived, how their society changed over time, and the various ways in which one might have experienced being Israelite in particular periods and settings.

The geographic and ecological parameters of Israel, the environments in which Israelites lived, are beautifully described by Michael Coogan (1998). Coogan has the reader picture the mild climate of the western portion of the Fertile Crescent, with its winter rains, summer heat, and fructifying rainy season from late fall to early spring (4). He then outlines the major topographic and geological zones in which Israel was located. The coastal plain, east of the Mediterranean, was "in antiquity wetter than now, even swampy in places, so that the main route to and from Egypt skirted it, occasionally hugging the foothills to the east (the biblical Shephelah, or 'lowland')." The coastal plain gradually rises through the foothills of the Shephelah eastward to the hill country of Judah, Ephraim, Galilee, and Lebanon. In antiquity, "the mountains of Lebanon were also densely forested with cypress and cedar. The rugged terrain...made travel difficult, except in the transverse valleys that lead through them from the coast to the Rift Valley" (5). The Rift Valley is "a deep gouge in the earth's surface that extends...from Southern Turkey into East Africa" (5). This valley leads down to the Dead Sea, the lowest elevation on earth. Coursing through the valley is the Jordan River, watering and making fertile the upper portion of the Jordan Valley; "south of the hill country is a marginal zone, the biblical Negeb, which merges with the Sinai Peninsula" (5). West of the Rift Valley is the abrupt "ascent to the plateau of the Jordan....The transjordan plateau lies slightly higher than the hill country west of the Jordan, and receives somewhat less rainfall—sufficient, however, for agriculture and for sheep and goat herding. It is also cut by several rivers" (5–7).

The ecosystems experienced by Israelites influenced the economy and way of life in various areas, perhaps also helping to shape gender roles, social structure, the distribution of power, aesthetic values, and hair customs. Israel's immediate neighbors, frequently mentioned in the Hebrew Bible sometimes as allies but more frequently as competitors, would have shared some of these fundamental environments. By the Early Iron Age (from the end of the thirteenth century BCE to the tenth century BCE), soon after the time of Israel's earliest named presence in the land (see below), the Philistines, who originated among the Sea Peoples of the Aegean, and the Phoenicians, seafaring Canaanites, occupied the coastlands of the Mediterranean to the west, while various Transjordanian groups were to the east. The Transjordanian peoples included the Edomites, the Moabites, and the Ammonites, all of whom spoke "Canaanite languages related to Hebrew and Phoenician" (Hackett 1998, 205). Biblical foundation stories place these groups in ancient genealogies shared by Israel, perhaps recognizing the love–hate relationship that characterizes the attempt to distinguish one's own group from neighbors who share much in terms of history, language, geography, and worldview. To the north of Ammon, northeast of Israel, lay Aram or Syria, an area politically organized into a kingdom by the time of the Israelite monarchy in the tenth century BCE. Like the Transjordanian groups, the Syrians or Aramaeans had much in common culturally and linguistically with Israel.

Representations in Egyptian art of Syrians or the other Semitic peoples are sometimes cited to suggest how Israelites might have worn their hair. One must wonder, however, if Israelites would have wanted to look like their neighbors. Would Egyptians have distinguished visually between Syrians and Israelites? Would these groups have worn their hair in imitation of one another or shared this hairstyle despite other cultural differences? Would northern Israelites have been more likely than their Judean kinsmen to wear their hair and beards like those of nearby Syrians?

Critical to an overview of Israel's surroundings are the superpowers of the area, Egypt, Assyria, Babylonia, and Persia, whose art depicts Israelites or their neighbors. Egypt, located to Israel's south, in the northeast of Africa and west of the Arabian Peninsula, is the biblical setting for tales of the patriarch Joseph and the exodus account. Although such accounts are deeply important reflections of Israelite worldview, they are not taken as historical events by most modern scholars (Redmount 1988). Nonetheless, Egypt was an important political and cultural force acting upon Syria-Palestine in the Late Bronze Age. As emphasized by Donald Redford (1992), the influence of Egyptian culture upon Israelite culture of various periods is often underestimated. A superpower of the eighth century BCE, Assyria of northern Mesopotamia conquered the northern Israelite kingdom and subdued the southern kingdom of Judah. Assyrian influence in art and culture, especially in the north, was significant in this period. A later conqueror was the southern Mesopotamian powerhouse Babylonia, responsible for the destruction of the southern kingdom of Judah in 587–586 BCE and the exile of its elites to Babylonia. Persia to the southeast of Babylon and across the Persian Gulf controlled a massive empire that at its height in 500 BCE spanned the ancient world from India in the east to Thrace in the west, just shy of Greece. Persia thus replaced Babylonia as the overlord of Israel in the late sixth century BCE. Some Israelite leaders of the Persian period held power directly from the Persian monarch. Each of these great civilizations produced art that reveals hairstyles of their own and their subjugated peoples, and each may have influenced the ways in which Israelites wore their hair or thought about their hair.

Israelite Social History: Biblical and Archaeological Versions

The discussion of Israel's neighbors and cultural influences already approaches the subject of Israelite history. Geographically, Israel was in a valuable, greatly desired part of the ancient Near East, an economic crossroads between east and west, the land a setting for wars, the people a frequent victim of conquest and subjugation. We know about Israelites from the references and commentaries of their enemies, for example, on victory steles, from archaeological evidence (inscriptions, everyday objects, and art), and from the richly complex, multilayered, multivoiced library of ancient Israelite literature, the Hebrew Bible. The Hebrew Bible tells us what its various composers and preservers thought of Israelite identity and history. The views are not uniform; the Bible was made and remade many times over many centuries, and many voices are represented. Nevertheless, certain writers got the last word in setting the essential contours of Israel's story, and an essential pan-Israelite view of history and identity emerges. There are, in other words, certain common denominators to which we will allude in the course of our study of hair. Questions about Israelite social history, identity, and self-definition become even more complex when archaeological data are included in the analysis. What follows is an attempt to cautiously and judiciously sketch the outlines of Israelite social history as relevant to writing about hair, culture, and group identity. It is useful to divide the history of Israel into three main periods: premonarchic, monarchic, and postmonarchic.

Premonarchic Period

A critical chronological marker for the emergence of Israel is a reference in the late thirteenth-century BCE victory stela of the Egyptian pharaoh Merneptah (or Merenptah). Merneptah describes his assumption of hegemony thus: "his land is laid waste." Scholars have debated whether the hieroglyph transliterated *ysry³r/l* actually should be read "Israel," but most agree that it should be read this way and that the term does refer to biblical Israel, with the connotation of a people named Israel, rather than a nation state (Kitchen 2004, 270–272). Scholars also debate about the geographic location of Merneptah's Israel (Killebrew 2005, 155), but the majority interprets the inscription to refer to the central highlands region (see Killebrew 2005, 154–155; Kitchen 2004, 272). In this way, an Egyptian source does seem to recognize the existence of Israel in an appropriate location by the end of the thirteenth century BCE.

The Hebrew Bible provides a store of engaging traditional-style tales about ancestor heroes and heroines, including patriarchs and matriarchs such as Abraham and Sarah and leaders such as Moses, Miriam, Aaron, Joshua, and Samson. Few scholars nowadays, however, would accept as historical, in a strictly or simply factual sense, the biblical versions of the lives of these premonarchic heroes or the events of exodus, the wandering through the wilderness, the conquest, and the period of the colorful leaders called "judges" that occupy the biblical books from Genesis 12 through Judges. Modern scholars do not, moreover, accept the boundaries of an early Israelite state offered by the Bible; indeed many contradictory maps are offered. Nor do scholars accept the historicity of a twelve-tribe nation whose progenitors are all sons of the patriarch Jacob, although the Israelites who wrote the Bible saw themselves and self-identified in terms of this genealogy, sharing a worldview in which kinship truly matters. However, if scholarly interpretations are correct, Merneptah does claim to have defeated this group called Israel in battle, and they do have an identity and setting in the view of the scribes of that Egyptian monarch.

Archaeologists and biblical sociologists paint the earliest period another way. By the thirteenth century BCE, Israelites and their linguistically related neighbors lived in central frontier highlands locations such as Ai, Bethel, Shiloh, and Raddana. It has been suggested that the Israelites, or those who would become the Israelites, came to these frontier areas from settled locations in response to the economic disruptions attending the "decline of the Late Bronze city-state, and in certain areas, of Egyptian imperial control" (Stager 1998, 142). The "ruralization hypothesis" pictures the early Israelites as ancient economic refugees looking for a new life. Lawrence Stager (1998) suggests that many of the settlers would have been herders who had formerly provisioned the vibrant populations of the city-states in their heyday. Farmers, former mercenaries, and nomads also may have been among the settlers, all of whom might have contributed to the cultural heritage and the customs of Israel.

Ann Killebrew (2005, 13) and other contemporary scholars increasingly use the term "ethnogenesis" to describe the process by which a group would emerge from the cultures of Canaan during this time of economic and political upheaval to self-identify as the descendants of Israel. Notions of ethnicity include such features as shared stories, material culture, food customs, views of the group's history, and aesthetics. Hair and stories and rituals involving hair relate to several of these categories and remind us that a study of Israelite hair is also a study of ethnicity.

The earliest settlement area gradually expanded "southward to the Judaean hill country and northward to the Galilee" (Finkelstein 1985, 81). The Israelites were pastoral and agrarian. They raised animals such as goats, cows, and sheep and grew crops including olives, dates, figs, cereals, and legumes. They established terraced plots around their highland villages. In contrast to their Philistine neighbors, who arrived and settled on the Mediterranean coast in the twelfth century BCE, they did not raise pigs, for pig bones have not been found in areas of Israelite settlement (Bloch-Smith 2003). Men and women worked hard in this life of subsistence agriculture. Would the men and women have wanted the hair out of their faces as they did their physical, backbreaking chores? Their homes, as archaeologists have been able to reconstruct, were simple, small four-roomed houses, fifty feet by thirty feet, including stalls for the animals with whom they shared their space (Stager 1985). Cooking might take place in a central courtyard, around which were clusters of houses that probably belonged to extended families or kinship groupings, who would share the land and the work (Stager 1985; Meyers 1997, 12–21). One might conjecture that kinship groups would unify for defense and that certain leaders or chieftains might emerge in this prestate culture.

The collective memories preserved in the Hebrew Bible are written in terms of divine promises and a covenant with Yhwh, God of the patriarchs; they tell of liberation from slavery in Egypt, express the interrelatedness of all Israelites, and describe tribal allotments in various areas of the land. Religious life is pictured in the Hebrew Bible in terms of sacrificial ritual with the patriarch of the family playing a central role. Certain early sacred spaces, such as Shiloh and Dan, are also portrayed before the time of the monarchy, with a role for priestly adepts such as Eli and Samuel. Archaeology does not fill out with complete confidence the biblical picture of the religious lives of Israelites. Intriguing discoveries in the settlement region include a circle of stones with a large stone purposefully located at the circle's eastern rim and an eighteen-centimeter bronze statuette of a bull, found in the Samarian hills (Mazar 1992, 350–351). Identification with specifically Israelite groups is not certain, however, and the precise significance of such seemingly sacred spaces and objects is not known.

Likewise, we cannot prove the veracity of any aspects of the ancient historiographic accounts, but we can suggest that some of the biblical stories are very old and that Israel saw itself in terms of these stories from premonarchic times. The poetic victory songs in Exodus 15 and Judges 5 may well date to the twelfth century BCE, a conclusion scholars have reached based on the orthography, syntax, and prosodic style of the literature. If our translation is correct, in fact, Judges 5 begins with a reference to the long hair of warriors. These poems are characterized by recurring formulaic language and conventionalized patterns of content in a style of composition that is comparable to that of orally composed works. They provide evidence of rich narrative traditions about heroes and their deeds, battles with and victory over enemies. These early poems, like many other works of the Hebrew Bible composed in a variety of traditional styles, may well be imitative of oral literature rather than orally composed, but ancient Israelites, like the Greeks, no doubt lived in a world in which oral communication and styles typical of oral composition were highly valued. Very few examples of actual Hebrew writing from this early period are extant, but Israel remained a largely oral world, even once writing was more common during the period of the northern and southern monarchies (see Niditch 1996).

The Monarchies

The Hebrew Bible describes the monarchy of the hero King David and his son Solomon as a kind of golden age when Israel was a united kingdom with a capital in Jerusalem, boasting important building projects such as the great temple.

The kingdom engaged in international trade and had standing armies and a court bureaucracy. A variety of prophetic works claiming to be written during the reigns of various kings suggest, moreover, that with the rise of kingship came the rise of the prophets, some of whom supported the reigning establishment, while others were decidedly subversive. Although most biblical descriptions of specific events during the various kingly reigns from the tenth to the sixth centuries BCE are not historically provable, there is relevant extrabiblical evidence that supports the historicity of some basic elements of the ancient Israelite tradition. For example, an Aramaean king describes his victories, specifically mentioning the "the king of Israel" and the "house of David," that is, the Davidic dynasty, in a ninth-century BCE Aramaic inscription found at Tel Dan of Galilee. Assyrian documents refer to the Northern Kingdom of Israel as "the House of Omri," the famous dynasty of the northern kingdom which split from the south in the late tenth century BCE. An Assyrian relief on an obelisk of the ninth century BCE, of interest to the present topic because it depicts hairstyle and headgear, portrays and names Jehu, king of Israel, while Assyrian reliefs of the eighth century BCE illustrate the defeat of Lachish of Judah, again providing depictions of the inhabitants of that city. Archaeology has also made major contributions to our understanding of the world experienced and inhabited by Israelites from the tenth to the sixth centuries BCE.

On the one hand, the way of life in the villages continued for the vast majority of people as in the period before there were kings. Archaeological evidence reveals the continued the popularity of four-roomed houses in clusters, suggesting kin-based social structures and the dominance of an agrarian rural economy. The participation in the creation and re-creation of oral traditions no doubt continues. On the other hand, from the tenth century BCE on, there is archaeological evidence for a new urban culture as well. Cities such as Jerusalem and Samaria were, according to Mazar (1992), examples of a metropolis. Such cities boasted stone buildings, hewn-block masonry, six-chambered gateways, casement wall systems, and city streets made of beaten earth or cobblestones. Beyond the capitals were regional administrative centers such as Hazor, Megiddo, and Lachish. The eighth and seventh centuries BCE reveal increased use of the technology of writing. Hundreds of ostraca—writing, usually in ink, on pieces of broken pottery—have been unearthed in the Northern and Southern kingdoms. Written remains most often deal with economic, administrative, or military matters. Altars have been found in Dan in the north and Beer-sheba in the south, and a small temple has been discovered in Arad of Judah (Mazar 1992, 494–477). Cultic paraphernalia, including cult stands, incense bowls, seven-sprouted lamps, and a variety of figurines, have been found at various sites (Holladay 1987, 265–266; 272–273). Of special interest to our study of hair are the hundreds of pottery female figurines found in the north and south and the graffiti on jars, perhaps dating to the eighth century BCE, found at Kuntillet ʿAjrud, a southern location about fifty kilometers from Kadesh Barnea. The latter depict human or humanlike figures. All of this evidence converges to suggest a world with skilled artisans, scribes, cultic personnel, government bureaucrats of various kinds, and a military.

One wonders whether the hairstyle or beard of a Jerusalemite associated with royalty would differ from that of a village farmer. Did priests at the great temple in Jerusalem wear their hair a certain way? Do the hairstyles on the female figurines reflect iconic conventions or the hairstyles worn by real women? Would hair customs in the Northern Kingdom, Israel, differ from those in the Southern Kingdom, Judah, just as their dialects of Hebrew appear to have differed? Would there be other local, perhaps tribal, differences? Could particular hairstyles differentiate prophets, priests, and kings? As noted by Bloch-Smith, certain identities may well be overlapping; a male, northern, priestly aristocrat, for example, may have had several identities at once (e-mail to the author, June 25, 2005). Which hairstyle with its implicit cultural signals might dominate his demeanor? How does archaeological evidence relate to what biblical writers reveal about hair? The same questions apply to the third period, which is also represented well archaeologically. Even scholars who are suspicious of the earlier dating of biblical material would agree that worldviews of the postmonarchic period are well represented in the writings of the Hebrew Bible and that many biblical authors lived in this last period in our chronology.

Postmonarchic Period

The Northern Kingdom was defeated by the Assyrians in 721 BCE and the elite of its population exiled, with Assyrian influences becoming apparent in architecture and design. The Southern Kingdom lasted until 587–586 BCE, when it was conquered by the Babylonians. The temple in Jerusalem was destroyed, the monarchy ceased, and the elites of Jerusalem exiled, leaving behind a local power vacuum. The Persian Empire, which replaced Babylonia as the ancient world's superpower, allowed exiles to return to the land in 538 BCE. By 515 BCE, a less sumptuous temple had been rebuilt, and a variety of parties vied for political and cultural control. A pro-Persian group supported by the superpower left an important stamp on the Hebrew Bible and on Judaism itself. They are what Morton Smith (1987) has called "Yahweh-aloners." Conservative, theocratic, and priestly in orientation, they outlawed intermarriage, insisted on the cessation of Sabbath work, held to strict notions about ritual purity, and approached their political enemies with utter intolerance. By the same token, their social conscience insisted upon care for the poor and weak, still reeling in the aftermath of the exile and its subsequent rupture of the social fabric.

Scholars have become increasingly sophisticated and complex in their approach to this important and formative, but in many ways difficult-to-reconstruct, period in Jewish political and social history. In terms of economic and social well-being, some argue that Jerusalem itself was greatly disrupted and reduced in the postexilic period (Carter 1992; Hogland 1992). Others, however, point to cultural continuity after the loss of political independence, with sites outside of Jerusalem such as Gibeon, Mizpah, and Bethel providing archaeological evidence not only of survival but of vitality. To be sure, a changing of the guard may have allowed for and encouraged new and multiple sources of political and economic power. A Persian period work such as Ecclesiastes provides evidence of a new middle class, a lively cash economy, and opportunities for acquiring wealth through trading activities in the Persian Empire (Seow 2007). The Hebrew Bible reveals a wide range of interest groups, each with a particular worldview and political loyalties. In addition to the pro-Persian group, whose stamp is to be found in works such as Ezra and Nehemiah, other groups were equally conservative religiously but virulently opposed to any foreign rulers. Some of these groups were apocalyptic in orientation, expecting an overturning of present reality and the establishment of God's kingdom on earth, with or without a Davidic leader. Indeed, as Jon Berquist (2006) has suggested, some intellectuals may have reached the conclusion that "Judean monarchic self-rule was mostly an evil enterprise that ended badly and that God desired to curtail it" (64). In the power vacuum created by Babylonian conquest, some landowners who were not exiled may have increased their fortunes and enjoyed their autonomy without the Jerusalem elites, resenting those who returned to claim hegemony. Some people of priestly, aristocratic descent appear to have formed alliances with these landed gentry early in the return, and there were, no doubt, varying priestly groups vying for power, as we still see at the time of the Maccabean revolt in the second century BCE. Some in the postexilic period such as the authors of Jonah and Ruth were more tolerant, cosmopolitan, and "assimilationist" in orientation than the writers of Ezra and Nehemiah, as Morton Smith has beautifully shown. The culture of the north, Samaria, and its considerable continuities with the culture of Judea have also been newly explored by scholars. Gary Knoppers (2006) has shown that the north was relatively stable and economically well off during the Persian period.

Finally, one must remember that most exiles remained in Babylonia, continuing to engage in a culturally rich Jewish environment while maintaining ties with the motherland. There were thus various power bases in and influences upon postexilic Judea, as well as developments over time and various competing worldviews. How would attitudes toward hair reflect some of this diversity and social complexity? How did the conquering superpowers portray hairstyles of Israelites, and did these foreign influences have a noticeable effect on attitudes toward or portrayals of hair in biblical literature and ancient Near Eastern art? Do artifacts found in Israel help to answer these questions? Can we find developments from earlier to later times in portrayals of and attitudes toward hair that reflect developments in Israelite culture and changing forms of self-definition?

2

Hair in the Material Culture and Art of the Ancient Near East

Objects

One's life is colored and affected by a host of interactions with everyday objects. Bourdieu (1984) has emphasized the importance of grooming and other customs pertaining to the body, the habitual toilette, as a marker of cultural and personal identity. Increasingly, scholars of religion have come to a new, richer appreciation of the importance of material culture to understanding people's deepest orientation to life. Thus, in the study of hair and identity in ancient Israel, it would be useful to begin by picturing the sorts of objects held, used, and regularly seen by Israelites in connection with their hair. As with hairstyles, there may well have been differences between objects used by the poor and the wealthy, by women and men, in one part of the ancient Near East or another, and in one period or another. To add to our difficulties, even though archaeologists over the years have unearthed a plethora of objects relating to hair care, the exact provenance and dating of these objects was not always recorded or ascertained or their archaeological record preserved by scholars of an earlier era. Thus, while Michal Dayagi-Mendels (1993) includes in her valuable catalogue to an exhibit of ancient Near Eastern cosmetic items a photograph of objects having to do with the hair, she indicated (e-mail to author, August 14, 2006) that it would be difficult to provide specific labels for each of the pins or combs because such information is not available for many pieces long held in the collection of the Israel Museum. Nevertheless, we can point to a few more recent well-recorded discoveries.

Numerous combs and hairpins, made of wood or more elegant ivory, have been unearthed throughout the ancient Near East. Evidence of head lice still clings to some of these ancient artifacts (see, e.g., Mumcuoglu and Zias 1988). One might imagine a person whittling a hairpin or a comb or someone producing many to sell in a local cottage industry. Bronze Age fillets have also been found, made of beaten gold and leather (John Holladay, personal communication, August 2003). Again, one can imagine a trajectory of expense, gold being worn by aristocrats, cloth by ordinary men. Dayagi-Mendels' catalogue (1993) includes examples of mirrors, perfume bottles, and other objects for the toilette.

One can envisage a wealthy woman pinning her hair, choosing an ivory piece with a pretty carved top, checking stray hairs in a mirror held perhaps by a servant. Would she cover up with headgear of some kind if going out in public? Perhaps in some locales it was the custom, in others not. She has also perfumed herself from a bottle, perhaps in waiting for her husband or lover. One can imagine a young man fixing a cloth fillet to his head before leaving his home. How long was his hair? How did he cut it, if at all? The Hebrew Bible mentions razors. Who might have used razors to shave the hair on head or body? Disembodied artifacts only go so far.

Artistic Renderings: Considerations and Comparisons

If we were studying hair and identity in the first decade of twenty-first century American culture, we would supplement the relevant written material and a full range of visual evidence by interviews with actual people concerning their hairstyles. We would observe activities at beauty salons, explore images in magazines, and watch television and movies, noting changes in hair customs from period to period. We would be aware that the culture of baby boomers in this regard differs from that of their children, and we would expect that wealthy New Yorkers might wear their hair differently from wealthy Texans or that people in the suburbs might have hair preferences different from those in the city. As Haven Hamilton, the fictional country western star of Robert Altman's *Nashville,* says to the long-haired hippie piano player, "Get a haircut. You don't belong in Nashville."

It is a complex matter to explore the meanings of hair mediated by visual art, even in contemporary, living cultures, as many of the case studies mentioned in chapter 1 indicate. Past cultures provide even greater challenges.

Margaret Miles (1985, 35) notes, "Neither theological texts nor religious images can provide information about the culture in which they were formulated apart from a reconstruction of the part they played in the verbal and non-verbal discourse of their time and place, in the totality of messages intended and received."

Like John Berger (1977), Victor Turner (1967), Mary Douglas (1966), and the many other contributors to the study of cultural symbols introduced in chapter 1, Miles (1985) reminds us that context is critical. Thus when we explore images of hair in Egyptian, Assyrian, or Persian art, we must ask about the original purpose and setting of a work, about the messages and meanings it was meant to convey, and about those who would have seen it. We need to think about the way in which such viewers might have responded to an image, about the emotions it was meant to evoke, about the cultural context and setting of the artists and the conventions of their craft, and about the status and role of the people portrayed. We do well to consider the connections between artists' portrayals and reality and the tension between iconic or formulaic conventions and individual artistic visions. Ancient art, moreover, often comes to us broken and battered, with once striking and vibrant paint now partially or completely faded, with portions crumbled. Pieces are now often viewed in the artificial confines of the British Museum or the Metropolitan Museum of Art, making it more difficult to imagine a first or second millennium BCE setting. The identity of various peoples portrayed is often debated by scholars.

Nevertheless, it seems appropriate to frame our study of Israelite hair with a chapter concerning ancient Near Eastern portrayals of hair in visual media, paying special attention to the possible portrayals of the hairstyles of Israelites and the peoples of neighboring cultures with whom Israelites interacted. Ancient Near Eastern art of various periods and cultures purposefully, conventionally, and frequently depicted members of diverse cultural groups, distinguishing between their ethnic identities via hairstyle and clothing, sometimes but not always providing written identifications or titles as well.

The representation of foreigners in ancient Near Eastern art might remind the modern viewer of the exhibits of the world's peoples often described as "exotic races" at the great world's fairs of the early twentieth century. Eric Breitbart (1997) has collected photographs of the 1904 St. Louis World's Fair, exploring profound questions about the colonialist and condescending portrayals of the "Other" and about the various cultural roles played by images of ethnic groups who were regarded as inferior to or under the control of the exhibitors. Breitbart notes that 2,000 native peoples were brought to St. Louis to serve as living exhibits. The photographs of these exhibits provided "one way of keeping society in order" (13), while in the image, "the human subject became an abstraction" (16). The same might be said of ancient representations of conquered or subjugated peoples. Breitbart notes further how some of the photographs sent a purposeful message about relative power and worth. A small Negrito was photographed next to a six-foot white American, for example, to send a clear message (Breitbart 1997, 57). One sees the same use of relative size in the imagery of the ancient Near East to connote status where the king towers above all others (see below on a bowing Israelite Jehu before the great Shalmaneser). Breitbart also points to the inaccuracy, sometimes purposeful, of the labels in which various Pueblo peoples are outfitted and displayed as Moqui and Zuni (75) and those said to be Pueblo are actually Maricopa (80). All of the "cliff-dwelling groups" are exhibited en masse (73–80). The popular photograph labeled "Moki Corn Festival" was "staged with several Santa Clara and Pueblo Indians" (80; see fig. 2). Breitbart's observations about displays at the St. Louis World's Fair warn us to be equally suspicious of ancient labels. He notes that images may or may not correspond to reality but that they have the power "to define how people think about the world" (30). Breitbart was able to interview visitors to the fair who were still alive, assessing the affect on midwestern viewers of these living exhibits of long-haired, variously dressed indigenous peoples of the world, exploring further the lasting affect of the photos.

FIGURE 2. Moki Corn Festival (Library of Congress no. 5787). Photograph by William H. Rau.

His work serves as a reminder to ask who would have seen the ancient images, in what context, and to what effect.

The art of the ancient Near East is overt in its representation of the Other as subordinate. The theme of many of these portrayals is subjugation, whether demeaning or more respectful of the enemy (see Porter 2003, 86, 89, 90, 91), as foreign rulers or their representatives bring tribute and pay obeisance to the conquering king or as rows of prisoners are shown shackled and enslaved after conquest by one of the superpowers of the ancient world. In the latter category is the Egyptian relief in limestone from the Medinet Habu pavilion dating to the first half of the twelfth century BCE. The relief represents six bound prisoners who are labeled with names of various northern peoples (Pritchard 1969 [hereafter cited as ANEP], plate 9; see also plates 7 and 8 for Libyans, Syrians, etc.). The prisoners are each in the same position, on their knees, hands bound behind their backs. The poses in profile and the position of the figures are typically conventionalized according to the particular artistic tradition. The recurring imagery is of consummate subjugation and emphasizes that the prisoners are the losers—indeed, that all bow before Pharaoh. Nevertheless, the heads of the figures are variously drawn to demarcate ethnic differences. The first figure on the left, a prince of Hatti, is smooth-cheeked, his "hair held by a fillet and extending in a single curl down below the shoulders" (ANEP, plate 9; see discussion in ANEP, 250). The second is a prince of Amor (= Amurru) who wears a beard and thick hair tied with a fillet so that the gathered collection of strands appears shoulder length and rounded. The third from the left is "a chieftain of the *tykry*," with beard and hat or helmet; the fourth bearded figure is a *šrdn,* one of the Sea Peoples, who wears a distinctive helmet with projectiles. The fifth figure is a chieftain of the *š[krš]* who wears a beard and long, stiff outward-reaching hair or a hat, held by a band in front. The sixth is a *trš,* another of the Sea Peoples, who wears a fitted cap (see discussion in ANEP, 250).

A beautiful example of the display of subjugated peoples from the Persian period is provided by the rows of tribute bearers, represented on the Apadana reliefs, on the west stairs of the Palace of Darius, and on the Palace of Ataxerxes I in Persepolis (fig. 3). Although the identity of the various bearers is not certain, comparisons with labeled representations allow for educated guesses. As Moorey (1988) notes, "twenty-three groups, excluding the Persians are shown in a processional frieze dressed in their national costumes" (40). The headgear and hairstyles of the tribute bearers distinguish them—for example, Scythians with their pointed hats and Assyrians with distinctive head treatments. These rows of delegations of foreign peoples, all bringing offerings to the Persian ruler, project the variety and vastness of the Persian Empire.

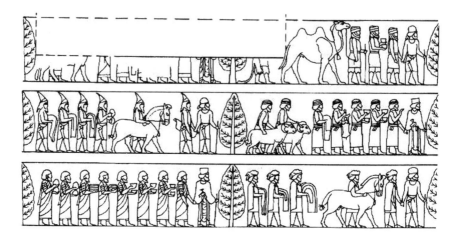

FIGURE 3. Tribute Bearers, Apadana reliefs. Courtesy of Cambridge University Press.

As we prepare for an examination of ancient Israelite hair, we will move chronologically through three main periods outlined in chapter 1 (premonarchic, monarchic, and postmonarchic), seeking out the ways in which ancient Near Eastern artists may have depicted Israelites and their neighbors. For the premonarchic period of the Late Bronze and Early Iron Ages, the major examples were produced by artists of Egypt, a superpower of the late second millennium BCE. A full appreciation of these depictions requires a brief introduction to Egyptian art of the era, to the worldview and aesthetic sensibility behind it, the training of artists, the materials used, and the presuppositions of its artists and expectations of audiences.

Egyptian Portrayals

Modern viewers of Egyptian art are probably first struck by its "nonperspectival" aspect. Scholars point to the intimate relationship between Egyptian art and Egyptian writing. Cyril Aldred (1980) suggests that pieces of art, which are usually accompanied by an inscription, are "ideograms writ large" and that hieroglyphs are "models for drawings on a larger scale" (15–18). Edna Russmann (2001) adds that the art was created in two dimensions on purpose and not because the Egyptians had not discovered perspective or were somehow visually primitive (28–29). Rather, the artist "represented...what he expected to exist for eternity...eternal verities" (Aldred 1980, 15). What was important was "the idea of objects rather than their exact realization in a spatial context" (18).

> The aim of the artists was to depict the enduring nature of objects and scenes they portrayed; they were not interested in how these might appear at any one time from a particular viewpoint. They used established conventions to encode the information they wished to convey.... A fundamental convention was that objects were shown in what was regarded as their most characteristic form, independent of time and space. (Robins 1994, 3)

Egyptian art has its own spatial integrity and proportions that "provide pattern and coherence to the whole" (Robins 1994, 11). "Images were not placed haphazardly on the drawing surface, unless there was a deliberate evocation of chaos, but were ordered by a system of registers" (Robins 1997, 21). In fact, a number of the portrayals of foreigners occur in scenes of battle in which the registers are purposefully violated, effectively invoking the intrinsic disorder and melee of war. In this case, purposeful violation of artistic formulas is the convention. Conventions are typical of and intrinsic to the traditional style of the art in which certain symbols stand for certain things. Comparisons with the formulaic qualities of oral literatures come to mind.

Aldred (1980) notes that depictions were not "peculiar to an individual artist, but (were) part of that immutable order of things" (15). Art was part of "the divine order charged with numinous power" (18). By the same token, the artist did not seek to produce exact copies of previous versions of one or another motif but, as in traditional-style literatures, produced variations upon the expected content and patterns (Robins 1997, 29). These conventions and the technical skills necessary to work in various media, such as limestone, calcite, and a variety of paints, were learned in artists' workshops, examples of which are depicted in Egyptian art (Robins 1997, 28). Artists worked in teams, and the production of monumental reliefs such as those at Karnak and Medinet Habu were major, well-organized collaborative efforts. Certain experts would first sketch out the contours of the relief on the surface of the stone wall, using brush and ink. Then sculptors would use chisels to carve out the depiction. Finally, artists, expert in the creation and application of appropriate colors, would paint the reliefs (Müller 2001, 134).

Reliefs carved into stone were either raised so that the stone background was cut away, a technique popular on inside walls, or sunk, so that figures were cut into the stone, leaving the background surfaces at a higher level, a technique used for outside walls. When one looks at photographs of the walls of Karnak or Medinet Habu, the pictures are difficult to make out, as the lines of content seem to blend into the host material. One has to remember, however, that these reliefs were originally painted in brilliant colors (see Aldred 1980, 28; W. S. Smith 1998, 217). Russman (2001) suggests that "Egyptian relief is best understood, in fact, as a means of reinforcing paint" (30). The use of bright paints explains how people could perceive the content of carved reliefs, which might be high up on a massive wall, and makes us imagine an aesthetic reality far different from that which survives today, preserved on site, in museums, or in photographs. Color, moreover, would have been essential to the depiction of hair and ethnicity. "Black pigment usually made from soot and sometimes from plumbago" was used to depict wigs and hair (Aldred 1980, 30). The shade of color chosen for skin, moreover, depicted gender and ethnicity (Aldred 1980, 30).

The works of art in great temples, palaces, or tombs "were produced for the elite and express their worldview" (Robins 1997, 18). One might say they were produced by elites for elites.

> The message of the relief and its inscriptions are primarily directed to the owner; they were not a medium of communication with the general population. The building inscription of Edfu says that priests and scholars should come to look at the temple and to admire the accomplishment of the king. As to the direct function of the relief, Egyptologists are not certain. What is clear, however, is that the reliefs make a political-theological statement about the king as leader of the world. The reliefs clearly confirm the consensus of the upper classes as to the role of the king as the preserver of creation. Overall, the buildings are a demonstration of the power and greatness of the ruler. (Müller, 132–133)

As Ulrich Luft (2001) notes, "In the New Kingdom (ca 1569–1076 BCE), the Egyptian who was not part of the priesthood could not directly participate in the rituals or enter the temple" (144). Thus the messages of the reliefs, while perhaps culturally shared by the population and reflecting the accepted worldview, did not operate like modern billboards to influence the general public. Iconic in nature, they encapsulated and made permanent a particular view of the world, helping to maintain and perpetuate that which they depict, such as the centrality of the king and his power over all enemies and forces of chaos.

Important in the study of hair are the portrayals of subjugated foreigners, who are always smaller than the conquering king. Commenting on glazed tiles from the palace of King Ramses III at Tell el-Yahudiya depicting bound Libyan, Syrian, and Nubian prisoners, Robins (1997) writes, "The figures are easily recognizable as foreigners by their non-Egyptian hairstyles and costume, which also serve to distinguish the different ethnic groups represented.

The representation of foreign prisoners in subjugation to the Egyptian king symbolized the king's role in maintaining the correct order of the universe by triumphing over the forces of chaos" (16).

Hair is integral to identity, whether Egyptian or foreign (Galpaz-Feller 2004), and a number of studies are devoted to Egyptian portrayals of Egyptian hair. J. L. Haynes (1977–1978) discusses the ways in which portrayals of women's hair in various dynasties reflect aesthetic developments and changing tastes, and "serve as a sound dating mechanism of female figures" (22). A. Lucas (1930) describes ancient Egyptian wigs, materials used, crafting techniques, and major styles, and approaches the wig as an important feature of ancient Egyptian material culture pertaining to hair. More broadly, Gay Robins (1999) and Saphinaz-Amal Naguib (1990) explore the ways in which portrayals of hair in ancient Egyptian art help to construct identity.

Naguib experiments with various methodological approaches and cross-cultural comparisons, while Robins closely analyzes portrayals of Egyptian hair within their cultural context. Both studies reveal the ways in which hairstyles reflect gender, age, and place in the social hierarchy: the side braids of some royal and elite young children versus the shaven heads of elite male adults who may wear shoulder-length wigs, and the long hair with sensual and sexual connotations, reaching to mid-chest, sometimes supplemented with wigs, for elite women (Robins 1999, 57; 59); the fact that sons are portrayed with shorter hair than their fathers in tomb paintings and sometimes wearing round wigs (Robins 1999, 59–60); the shaven heads of priests, emphasizing purity concerns; the preference for the beardlessness of men except for the false beards of kings and portrayals of gods (Naguib 1990, 16); the shaven heads of indoor male servants who do not wear wigs; the hair in natural, unkempt condition for outdoor servants (Robins 1999, 62; 67). Naguib also shows how hairstyles contrast Egyptians with foreigners. Drawing comparisons with imagery from the tale of Sinhue, an exiled Egyptian courtier, she notes that "Egyptians liked to represent themselves as 'hairless,' clean-shaven except in moments of crisis. On the other hand, foreigners were often depicted as 'hairy' and bearded" (Naguib 1990, 11; see also 16). Egyptian art provides us with the only possible pre-monarchic portrayal of Israelites.

A potential source of a premonarchic depiction of Israelite heads is one of the battle scenes preserved at the great complex of temples of Karnak, located by the Nile River, at the site of ancient Thebes. Gerald Kadish (2001) writes of the history of this site, "ruler after ruler trumpeted both piety and military success by adding to or rebuilding part of the complex while covering its walls with scenes and inscriptions of military victories, religious ceremonials, etc." (224).

The particular scene of interest is one of four on the western wall of the "Cour de la Cachette." For many years, scholars attributed the scenes to Rameses II, but more recently Frank J. Yurco (1990, 1997) proposed that the original cartouches dated from the reign and career of Merneptah, the same ruler whose thirteenth-century BCE victory stela mentions Israel by name. Yurco concludes for a variety of reasons that the scenes on the relief correspond to the names of groups who are said to be vanquished on the stela. If one accepts his identification, then one register (see fig. 4) provides a portrayal of Israelite warriors. Not all scholars agree with Yurco's identification of the enemy as Israelite or accept the association with the victories of Merneptah. Moreover, the relief is damaged, and we need to imagine it as brightly painted with clear contours marked in contrasting color. Again, one must emphasize the difficulties involved in deriving information about material culture from ancient art and in matching ancient art with biblical material. Regardless of the identity of the enemy, however, it is clear how small the enemy foes are in relation to the huge, majestic Egyptian horse. Scores of defeated men, arranged in a chaotic pile evoking the mayhem of battle, fit under the plane created by the steed's belly and legs. The message about relative strength and worth is clear. The hair of each enemy soldier is tied with a fillet and is full. It reaches to the shoulders in a rounded off shape and perhaps reflects the thickness and texture of the hair, indicating that the long hair has been gathered in a shoulder length pile via the fillet in order not to interfere with martial activities. The men are clearly bearded. If indeed the identification of the men as Israelite is correct, the style

FIGURE 4. Relief of Merneptah at Karnak, upper register. From the late thirteenth century BCE. Drawing and reconstruction: copyright L.E. Stager, with F. Yurco.

of their hair and beard is the same as those of the more confidently identified Canaanites of Ashkelon represented in the second register of the relief (see King and Stager 2001, 270). We can assume, therefore, that Egyptians associated the two groups by ethnic hairstyles. The Egyptians themselves are pictured as smoothly shaven, which corresponds with other evidence of their portrayals of Egyptian men's hair, discussed above (Yurco 1997, 39).

Although the identity of Israelites on the relief at Karnak is not certain, Israel's neighbors, the Syrians, are frequently portrayed and easily identified in Egyptian art. The Syrians were a Semitic people located in the area surrounding Damascus and speaking the Aramaic language, which is closely related to biblical Hebrew. Threads in the Hebrew Bible, in fact, suggest ancient ethnic connections—for example, "a wandering Aramean was my father" (Deuteronomy 26:5). Regardless of the degree that such reflections relate to historical reality, they do suggest, at least, that group memories were created or preserved concerning the relationship between the two peoples. The Egyptians portrayed Syrian hairstyles in ways that suggest their own view about the ethnic affinity of Syrians with Canaanites and perhaps with Israelites, if indeed Karnak portrays Israelite warriors. The classic Egyptian portrayal of Syrians pictures them with beards and shoulder-length, bushy hair held back with a fillet, with a length of the hair-tie hanging down at the back. The similarity to the hairstyles of the Cannanite and/or Israelite warriors in the relief at Karnak is clear. This hairstyle is found in fifteenth and fourteenth century BCE portrayals of Syrians (see ANEP, plates 47–52) and, closer in date to the emergence of Israel, thirteenth and twelfth BCE century portrayals (ANEP, plates 54, 55, 344, 346, 347).

Interesting in these arrays of Syrians are the variations in hairstyles, for some men, although bearded, are completely bald or shaven (see, for example, ANEP, plates 49, 50). It is important to mention that the bald men, who are interspersed with men with full heads of hair, are among captured prisoners or those offering tribute in a subjugated status. Is the implication that some of the captives or those who act out their inferior status in gift- giving have been made to shave in order to rob them of their identity or transform them? Have they been made to look more childlike, less like proper men within their own cultures, or to appear more like Egyptian male house servants? Are they being assimilated into Egyptian culture? Are some simply bald to indicate their advanced age? Why not portray all captives as bald? Could it be that portrayal of the expected Syrian hairstyle on some figures is necessary to mark ethnic identity? In reliefs at Medinet Habu, all the Syrians in the portrayals of their defeat by Rameses III have full hair and are bearded (see the warriors [ANEP, plate 344], and the lancers with full beards and hair tied with a fillet [ANEP, plate 346; fig. 5]). In this case, all still have their hair when presented as prisoners

FIGURE 5. Relief at Medinet Habu. Lancers defend a walled fortress in Amor from the forces of Ramses III (P. 18327/N. 10738). Courtesy of the Oriental Institute of the University of Chicago.

in a subsequent relief of the sequence (see ANEP, plate 347). Nevertheless, the baldness of some of the Syrians portrayed by some artists in Egyptian art may be a meaning-rich convention of some kind.

Another interesting variation is presented by one figure, a Syrian prisoner portrayed on a glazed tile from the period of Rameses III. This Syrian prisoner has the expected hair treatment with fillet, but no beard (King and Stager 2001, 268). Did some Syrians not wear beards? Was his beard imagined to have been removed as a kind of humiliation for a defeated enemy who projects his manhood culturally through facial hair? Again, is he being assimilated into Egyptian culture, or does the artist simply get the archetype wrong, equating him with the nearby Libyan who would have been smooth shaven? Perhaps these variations in hair are indicators of body politic, like the imposition or removal of the queue in periods of Chinese social history.

One other variation involves the shape of Syrian beards as portrayed by Egyptians. Some are quite stylized and pointy, as if cut to a certain shape, while others are full and flow more naturally (see ANEP, plate 55 for a fuller beard and plate 53 for a pointed beard). It is unclear whether such variation is arbitrary, an indication of status, or a matter of artistic aesthetics and preference. In any event, it is clear that hairstyle connotes ethnicity, that Syrians, in the minds of Egyptians, shared ethnicity with their Canaanite and perhaps Israelite neighbors, and that the portrayals of these foreigners allowed for some variation. These variations are no doubt related to Egyptian views of the defeated Syrian Other, to the way Syrians viewed themselves, and to the way in which Syrians really wore their hair. Interpretation is difficult.

The bearded, long-haired Syrian, Canaanite, and perhaps Israelite warriors compare in important ways with Egyptian depictions of another early Iron Age enemy of the Israelites, the Philistines. The sources are reliefs at Medinet Habu, found more specifically in an area near the southern end of the Theban acropolis. The great temple that memorializes the activities of Rameses III (r. 1198–1166) includes reliefs depicting the wars of that ruler against the Sea Peoples, among whom are the Philistines who gained control of the Mediterranean coast to the west of Israel's settlement region. The Sea Peoples became a formidable military challenge to Egyptian power in the twelfth century BCE. Donald Redford (2000) suggests that "The Medinet Habu artists and sculptors witnessed, most likely directly, the prospect of strangely-clad captives from the Aegean and Asia Minor paraded before Pharaoh. These they reproduced as faithfully as they could" (12).

David O'Connor (2000) notes that the various Sea Peoples are distinguishable from each other through their headdresses. The "'feathered or reed helmet' is associated with Peleset" (Philistines) and other groups. "Generally, the Sea Peoples are beardless (as compared, for example, with Levantines)" (85). Ann Killebrew (2005) states that the only warrior who is clearly labeled as "Philistine" in ancient Egyptian art is in fact bearded (15, 202), but the view of most scholars is that Philistine warriors generally looked much like the falling, chaotically arranged soldiers in the depictions of the victorious battles on land and sea of the Egyptian Rameses III and in scenes of chained groups of prisoners from these battles (see figs. 6 and 7; Wachsmann 2000, 110–113; Stager 1998, 159; O'Connor 2000, 96; 98). Notice the stylized, fluted hat or hair that some scholars have regarded as plumes, reminiscent of the birds on the prows of Egyptian ships. Others have suggested that some material—stiff, folded cloth or reed—accounts for the look.

Elizabeth Bloch-Smith (2003) and Lawrence Stager (1998) have each shown how hairstyle and head treatment are ethnic identifiers, distinguishing

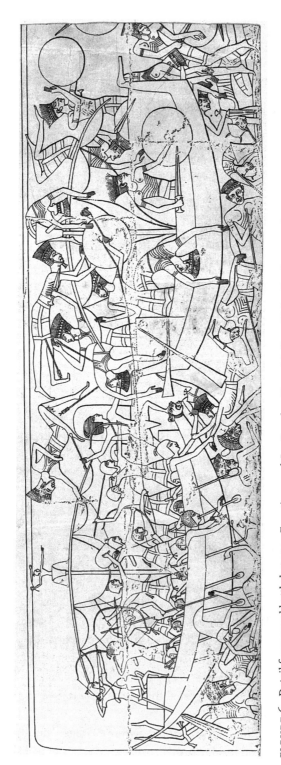

FIGURE 6. Detail from naval battle between Egyptians and Sea Peoples. From Medinet Habu (P. 16342/N. 18499). Courtesy of the Oriental Institute of the University of Chicago.

FIGURE 7. A slain Philistine, relief from Medinet Habu (P. 16338/N. 18486). Courtesy of the Oriental Institute of the University of Chicago.

Philistine from Israelite. Stager brings to bear evidence from excavations of the ancient Philistine city of Ashkelon. There archeologists have found broken pieces of a Philistine bichrome krater or drinking vessel that provide the first self-portraits of Philistine warriors (fig. 8; Stager 1998, 164; King and Stager 2001, 229). These figures, which Stager (1998) describes as cartoonlike, display a feathered or spiked headdress or hairstyle, and the heavily outlined faces are without beards and thus resemble the more elegant and stylized portrayals of soldiers and seamen from Medinet Habu. Significantly, they also closely resemble the portrayals of sailors and warriors on Mycenaean pottery, supporting suggestions about the Aegean origins of the Philistines, and further suggesting that indeed the Philistines were clean shaven and that military men wore distinctive hair or head treatments.

Israelite Artists?

In 1975–1976 a team of Israeli archeologists excavated at Kuntillet 'Ajrud, a site in the Sinai about fifty kilometers south of Kadesh Barnea, near the intersection of several ancient trade routes. They unearthed the remains of two buildings and found a number of important inscriptions and drawings that scholars have dated to the late ninth or early eighth century BCE. Some scholars have suggested that the site reveals an ancient sacred space, a cultic center, and one suggested the presence of a school, but the current consensus is that the

FIGURE 8. Pieces of a Philistine biochrome krater depicting warriors. Courtesy of the Leon Levy Expedition to Ashkelon.

buildings mark a way station or caravanserai visited by travelers on one or another of the trade routes (Hadley 2000, 106–114). Keel and Uehlinger (1998) suggest that this "caravanserai was a royal/state outpost, a trade route that was under government control" (246). They, McCarter (1987), and others suggest, moreover, that northern Israelites were the controlling force at this period. One of the inscriptions at the site, drawn on a large storage jar or pithos (see fig. 9), reads in part "I bless you by Yahweh of Samaria and by his Asherah," leading to speculation about the nature of Israelite religion, the possible presence of a goddess as consort to a male Yahweh, and about the role of particular iconic representations of the deity. A detailed discussion of the implications of the inscription would take us too far afield. However, this pithos and another large storage jar (see fig. 10) also include drawings, painted in red, of human or humanlike figures that have particular treatments of the head and/or hair. The drawings pose difficult methodological problems, but, as this site is generally regarded as having an Israelite connection, it seems incumbent upon us to explore the drawings for possible information.

FIGURE 9. Drawing on large storage jar from Kuntillet ʿAjrud. Courtesy of Professor Zeev Meshel.

The faces of the two standing figures appear to have cowlike features. Each stands in an upright position, and a tail or perhaps a phallus hangs down between the legs. The smaller figure in the center may have breasts indicated by the small circles on the chest. Due to the relative size of the figures and the pose, with the larger figure (without the breast markings) standing in front, some scholars have suggested that these figures represent "Yahweh and his Asherah," mentioned in the inscription on the pithos, although Beck (1982) doubts that the two figures represent a male–female couple (31). She (1982: 29) and others have drawn comparisons with ancient Near Eastern portrayals of Bes figures— Bes being "the name usually given to a group of Egyptian dwarf gods" (Hadley 2000, 137), although there is debate among scholars concerning this identification. The large array of types of Bes gods does allow scholars to locate some features of the iconography (see Beck 1982, 27–31; Keel and Uehlinger 1998, 246–252). The headdresses are of special interest to the present study.

The figure on the left of the pithos wears spiked headgear, which Beck (1982) calls a "feathered headdress" (29). The three protuberances remind one of horns or ears of grain. The figure to the right wears a small crownlike headdress in the middle of the head. Both headdresses have been linked to portrayals of Bes figures (Hadley 2000, 139), although these include a wide array of iconic conventions, and the small crown is not typical of the headgear of Bes figures (Beck 1982, 31). The seated figure at the lyre is also of indeterminate gender. Hadley (2000) agrees with Dever (1984, 22) that the dots on the head of the figure "denote(s) either a long wig or a coiffure of tight curls or ringlets" (149). Hadley concludes that the dots betoken a "typical Egyptian-type wig or hair covering for men" (148), whereas Beck (1982) relates the dots to "the decorative tradition of 'Midianite' pottery of the end of the second millennium" (34).

The figures indicate a very eclectic, cosmopolitan, multicultural aesthetic, which may well be appropriate for a caravanserai visited by people from various areas of the ancient Near East. As Hadley (2000) notes, "the site would be available to anyone of any ethnic background, who passed that way for any reason" (116). She has us picture among the weary travelers "pilgrim, prophet, soldier, merchant, or herdsman" (120). Such head treatments may have been drawn by an Israelite or perhaps a Phoenician or a person of some other ethnicity, familiar with the sort of motifs reminiscent of Egyptian iconography (see Keel and Uehlinger 1988, 259). Beck (1982) notes that "A complex cultural background emerges for the painters of the lyre player and Bes figures. These may not have been the most skillful artists, but they were certainly familiar with both Phoenician and North Syrian iconography and the 'desert art' of Arabia and the Negev" (36).

Would the hairstyles portrayed be found in the repertoire of actual people? Do they perhaps reflect the exotic hairstyles of some groups? One thinks here of the magnificent ornate hairstyles of various African cultures explored in our first chapter. Who would have drawn such figures? They do not reflect the skill of the Egyptian artists, discussed above. The portrayals seem more in the nature of graffiti or quick, temporary, moveable art. As Beck (1982) notes, the pithoi "were decorated spontaneously after firing" (36), once the vessels were already in their present location. Someone perhaps rather quickly brought them into this border place as a kind of protection; they may have operated visually as the inscriptions did verbally. One thinks of the region's magical bowls of a much later period with inscriptions and quick, crude drawings (see Naveh and Shaked 1985, bowls 9 and 11, plates 25 and 27). The art on the second pithos is even more suggestive of quickly drawn graffiti (see fig. 10). The hair is again of special interest.

These figures appear to be men, standing with upraised arms in prayer or supplication. The graffito was not finished. Some heads lack bodies, some bodies are incomplete, and some lack hair. The full figures, however, are beardless and have the spiked or feathered hair we have seen in the Philistine krater from Ashkelon. Such stick figures are perhaps virtually universal in the human repertoire, but the lack of beards might be significant in a world in which men always wore beards. Beck relates the hairstyle to the kind of free, natural hair design worn by the nomadic herder, portrayed on the Egyptian Tomb of Meir of the twelfth dynasty (ANEP, plate 101; Beck 1982, 39–40), but the hair of the

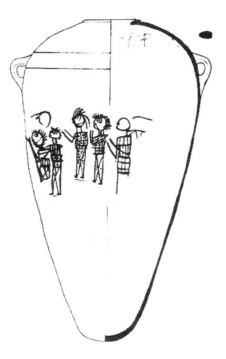

FIGURE 10. Drawing on a large storage jar from Kuntilet ʿAjrud. Courtesy of Professor Zeev Meshel.

nomad is much fuller and not depicted in strands, and he is bearded. In any event, as in the case of the first pithos, a multicultural aesthetic is at play, and the possibility exists that the creator of the figures was from one of a variety of ethnicities or exposed to a variety of hairstyles.

The buildings at Kuntillet ʿAjrud also contain fragments of relevant paintings in red, yellow, and black that were brushed onto plastered walls. A few human figures can be reconstructed or discerned. Two of the clearest, seen in profile, are part of a seeming battle scene and are perched upon a city wall. One wears a pointed helmet, perhaps with long hair hanging out at the back, and the other, pictured with a slightly smaller head, has a rounded, close-fitting hat or helmet. Beck (1982) considers these conventionalized representations to be "part of the stock-in-trade of the Phoenician artisans" (49).

The figures at Kuntillet ʿAjrud, then, do not reveal information about Israelites' self-portrayals pertaining to hairstyle, but they do reveal some of the eclecticism and the globalist aesthetic at play in a portion of the early Iron Age world to which the Israelites of the monarchies belonged. Those taking long journeys would participate in and be exposed to this ethnic and aesthetic diversity.

Another possible resource for representations of hair in the period of the monarchy is offered by the hundreds of Judean female "pillar-figurines" generally dated to the Iron Age II, circa ninth to seventh centuries BCE. Almost half of the finds were distributed in the Jerusalem area, and the rest were found in various sites including Ramat Raḥel, Tel Nabesh, Arad, Beer-sheba, Gezer, Lachish, and Gibeon (see fig. 11; Kletter 1996, 97). The figures have a hollow, "pillar" type base, which constitutes the "body" of the figure, upon which is a woman's head. Many of these artifacts, designed according to certain aesthetic conventions or formulaic content, have survived only in pieces. Of relevance for our study is a type of molded face that is adorned with variations upon a particular style of headdress. The face is surrounded on three sides by curls. Kletter (1996) writes, "There are as many as six ridges with rows of curls above the forehead.... The curls vary in shapes, and the variations of the number of rows enable a detailed typology. Usually there are protruding side-locks, descending to the chin but never further down. Use of white-wash and painted decoration in yellow and red is common" (20).

The shape and length of hairstyle of these figurines compare well to the representation of hair on the head of a "bottle figure," an ivory flask from Lachish, shaped like a standing woman and dating from the twelfth century BCE (see Barnett 1982, plate 21a). The convention and perhaps the actual hairstyle is an old one in the area.

FIGURE 11. Judean pillar figurines. Courtesy of the Israel Antiquities Authority.

Another common type of female figurine found in coastal and northern Israelite areas was usually more elaborate than the Judean figurines. On these pieces, "long side-locks reaching shoulders or the neck at least" (Kletter 1996, 32) are common. Also of note are figurines found in Phoenician areas on the coast, exhibiting perhaps other preferences for hairstyle or at least for artistic conventions for portraying women's hair. In these, "hair is collected in long side-locks often ending with a large 'bun' or 'earlobe' shape on the shoulders. In other cases the side-locks are twisted" (Kletter 1996, 35).

These images of women's hairstyles raise questions about their relationship to actual women or to the ethnic identity of those who owned the figurines. One needs to ask as well about the function of these figurines, their symbolic meaning, if any, and about their origins. Are they imports, reflecting another culture's conventions concerning the representation of women's hair, or local products? Of course, even local products can incorporate an international set of conventions that may or may not reflect the styles of real women's hair.

Raz Kletter (1996) offers possible answers to some of these questions. It does appear that the figurines were locally made from local clays, and they appear to have been mass produced from a limited number of molds; they were not expensive objects (41, 69). Variations could be incised on the clay by hand, for example, to indicate strands of hair (51). They have been unearthed "in all types of contexts, or at all levels of human activity, and especially in the daily domestic realm" (62). Kletter outlines possible identities, meanings, and functions of the figurines: (1) toys; (2) representations of mortal women; (3) representations of goddesses, either a generalized "earth mother" or more specifically and likely in Kletter's view, an Asherah figure; and (4) a figure used in magic. We have discussed Asherah, possible consort to Yahweh, in connection with the images of Kuntillet 'Ajrud above. Kletter and most scholars regard these figurines as representations of Asherah functioning in daily religion as lived as a "protecting figure in domestic houses, more likely a figure which bestowed 'plenty,' especially in the domain of female lives (but not necessarily used by women only)" (81). The function of Asherah is "magical" in that her presence as one associated with fertility helps to confer fertility on her household.

Would actual Israelite women wear their hair in the style of any of these figures? Were the various hairstyles represented on the figurines available to all women of the general geographic area, as we saw in evidence from African cultures, where women would try their neighbors' hairstyles and not necessarily conform to one limited style all the time? It is difficult to know. The tightly curled short hairdo visually has more in common with Assyrian representations of some of the men defeated in the battle for Lachish in the eighth century BCE than with earlier Egyptian portrayals of Canaanites, possible Israelites, and Syrians, but this is not to suggest direct influence of Assyrian art or their images of their neighbors' hairstyles. The heads of Judean women are covered in the Lachish reliefs. A shorter hairdo would make sense if the Nazirite vow (Numbers 6) required women to grow their hair long. In contrast, the image of long-haired figurines corresponds better with the idealization of the young woman in Song of Songs and with the priest's letting the woman's hair go free or flow long in the ritual for the woman accused of adultery (Numbers 5). In any event, the figurines do provide some evidence of the interest in hairstyle held by artists and their customers in the Iron Age and of the variations that were possible in the repertoire.

One more possible Judean portrayal of a Judean is offered by the eighth century BCE sherd discovered at Ramat Raḥel, about halfway between Jerusalem and Bethlehem. The figure on a small piece of pottery measuring five by three inches was drawn in red and black, colors which have now greatly faded on the original artifact (see Barkay 2006, 42–43; King and Stager 2001, 260). Sitting on a throne, the figure has shoulder-length hair painted in neat stylized locks, and a pointed, neatly shaped beard juts from his chin. The top of the sherd is broken so that we cannot see his headgear. Geva (1981) suggests Greek influence on a Judean artist, but others see the drawing as somewhat like figures in Assyrian art preserved at Arslan-Tash in northern Syria (see Barkay 2006, 44). Barkay believes the drawing represents a "Judahite king" (43), perhaps Hezekiah. The pointed beard is similar to some of the pointed beards of Syrians in Egyptian art (see ANEP, plate 53)

In any event, the painting may well be an example of a Judean representing a Judean in the eighth century BCE. The man is well-dressed, and his hair and beard are well-tended and styled to be a certain shape. He may exemplify aesthetic taste among Judean elites of a certain place and period.

Assyrian Portrayals of Northern Israelites and Judeans

In contrast to the pillar figurines and the figures painted at Kuntillet ʿAjrud, Assyrian reliefs portray human beings that are actually labeled so that we can ascertain that they are meant to be Israelite, northern or southern. The ninth century BCE Black Obelisk, a stele of Shalmaneser III, depicts the northern Israelite King Jehu bending and bowing in obeisance to the Assyrian monarch, while panoramic eighth century BCE reliefs from the Palace of Sennacherib at Nineveh depict the defeat and subjugation of the Judean city Lachish and its inhabitants. Both men and women appear, and there is some interesting variation in the treatment of hair and headdresses.

Like other depictions, Assyrian portrayals of hair need to be considered in context, including the art of the period, its style and conventions; artisans' knowledge of actual Israelites and related questions about the realism of the portrayals; the composition of the audience of the reliefs; questions concerning ethnicity and identity; and the purpose of the portrayals. As in dealing with all of these products of the ancient world, we also have to remember that the images that have been preserved may not be exactly as they were in the ninth or eighth centuries BCE. We rely on drawings, for example, of the Lachish reliefs made on site by nineteenth-century artists. These renderings often reconstruct or make best guesses about what has been damaged by ancient armies or by the ravages of time. Even the original pieces have undergone reconstruction before being displayed in museum settings, and what constitutes the most correct arrangement of works, such as the various slabs of the Lachish panorama, is debated by scholars (see Russell 1998; Uehlinger 2003, 268–273).

As in Egypt, Assyrian designs for reliefs were "drawn in outline" before they were carved. A letter to Ashurbanipal suggests that the king himself oversaw the plans and gave approval before the project proceeded. The king was clearly invested in the project. The quality of the carving varies. The method used was to sketch the design in ink, then cut away the background stone. Surface detail could then be incised (Moorey 1994, 34–35). In the various beards and hair, we see both incised, surface carving, and more ornate shaping requiring greater sculptural skill. The stone used in reliefs in Sennacherib's palace was mostly gypsum and some fossiliferous limestone (Moorey 1994, 344–345). P. R. S. Moorey (1994) also suggests that some or part of the reliefs may have been painted, but it is difficult to ascertain the role of color due to the condition of the reliefs that have survived (35).

To see the reliefs as the Assyrians saw them, one needs to understand the conventions at work in the culture. As Winter (1981) notes, "the ability to receive the message contained in the program...is a direct function of the effectiveness and clarity of the presentation of the message" and depends upon "the cognitive competence of the audience: the stored knowledge brought to the situation, ability to understand signs and signals, and skill in decoding" (29). Conventions employed by artists and expected by audiences reflect and help shape identity and are critical to self-recognition. Many of these conventions pertain to the head and hair: various sorts of head covering for men and women, the bent, soft pointy hat of Jehu, the pointed helmet with side-flap worn by some of Lachish's defenders, the head-fitting helmet, cloth wrap, or hat with side-flap worn by male adults and boys leaving the exiled city as prisoners and refugees; the long headgear of captured women and girls; the treatment of men's facial hair in the Lachish reliefs, both the beards conveyed by incised lines on the chin and cheek and the curled, crisp short hair and beards, more like portrayals of the hair of North Africans. In fact, the ethnic identity of the male victims with crisply curled hair and beards at Lachish is considered to be Judean by most scholars including Barnett (1958; 1960), Russell (1991; 1993), King and Stager (2001), Dayagi-Mendels (1993), and Wäfler (1975) but others, including Julian Reade (1999), Pauline Albenda (1982), and Dominique Collon (1985), have suggested that the prisoners with crisply curled hair may be Nubian or Egyptian. I return to this specific debate later, but first I explore a valuable general framework offered by Megan Cifarelli (1998) concerning identity and otherness in Assyrian art.

Cifarelli (1998) shows the ways in which conventionalized gestures, postures, dress, and hair treatment not only indicate "ethnic or geographic origins" but also send messages concerning "relative status," demarcating who is dominant and who is dominated (214). These roles are meant to be perceived as deserved. Cifarelli writes, "One of the tenets of the ideology expressed and formulated through the art of Ashurnasirpal...was a negative conception of alterity, of the *otherness* or cultural difference ascribed to foreigners. In this system, the features that distinguish non-Assyrians from Assyrians were understood to be sinister and abnormal" (211; emphasis in original). Key gestures and features conveying this inferior otherness include the exposure of legs of women captives to portray them as objectified and immodest, the grasping of defeated enemies' hair, particular haircuts worn by the Other, and the crouching position and raised hands that indicate subservience within this system of conventions.

A close examination of the portrayal of Jehu before the figure of Shalmaneser III reveals, in particular, the posture of obeisance described by Cifarelli (1998). Jehu is carved in the second of four bands of reliefs on one of the four sides of the obelisk (fig. 12). The characters appear in a horizontal, profiled, perspective-free manner typical of larger reliefs before the time of Sennacherib, and "all figures are on a single ground line" (Russell 1993, 57). The obelisk, sculpted in a dark limestone, would have been set up in a public area. On the one hand, Reade (1999), like Porter (2003), reminds us that not all such portrayals of foreigners were meant to intimidate in an overt, brutal manner, but "insist rather on the pacific nature of the ninth-century Assyrian empire" (Reade 1999, 23). They show "the desirable after-effects of successful power politics," as "the king appears receiving the tribute of a submissive world" (23). On the other hand, Jehu is the consummate crouching tributary, the conquered ruler who is put in his place. His gaze is downward toward the king's feet or the earth itself, his beard touches the ground as his hands clutch the ground beneath him for support. As Cynthia Chapman (2004) has noted, "Bowing and kissing the feet of

FIGURE 12. Jehu crouching in obeisance. Black Obelisk of Shamaneser III (BM 118885). Copyright Trustees of the British Museum.

the Assyrian king or even the ground in front of the Assyrian king signaled the surrender of a foreign king. Of course, this action also constituted forfeiture in the masculine contest of war" (39). Chapman also points to the significance of the beard's brushing the ground in front of the king or his feet as a symbol of the defeated enemy's "compromised masculinity" (39).

Jehu's back forms a diagonal downward from rear to front. His head treatment is also significant in creating an image of otherness. Cifarelli (1998) notes that "non-Assyrians from the Phoenician coast, for example, are generally depicted wearing soft caps" (213; see also Wäfler 1975, 72). Note Jehu's soft cap with the point bent back, like a kind of hunting cap. In June 2006, Dominique Collon pointed out to the author that the style of the cap of Jehu and various tribute bearers on the Black Obelisk is also found on workmen quarrying stone, portrayed in Court VI, panels 66–67 from the southwestern palace of

Sennacherib at Nineveh (700–692 BCE) and is worn by conquered peoples leaving under armed escort in the portrayal of the capture of Asartu from the reign of Tiglath Pileser (730–727 BCE; see Reade 1999, 64, fig. 68). Collon suggested that these hats signify "foreigner" or, in Cifarelli's terms, "alterity." Could the soft bent hat of Jehu be purposefully contrasted with Shalmaneser's stiff, erect headgear? Jehu's beard, shorter and less full than that of Shalmaneser, further reflects his subordinate status. As Irene Winter (1997) observes about portrayals of Assyrian monarchs, the coded message of the king's full beard is one of manliness, maturity, and power. He is "like the dominant male in a pride of lions with his generous mane" (Winter 1997, 371; see also Chapman 2004, 26; 39; 47). Messages about relative status and alterity are found as well in the eighth-century Lachish reliefs from the palace of Sennacherib at Nineveh.

Sennacherib's reliefs reveal exciting artistic innovation. Portrayals are not confined to horizontal registers but fill the "entire surface of the slab," allowing for "perspectival and narrative exploitation" (Russell 1993, 60). Sennacherib's artists eliminate the central band of text that separated the visual surface into thinner horizontal lines of narration. "Unlike the inflexible register divisions in the reliefs of his predecessors, Sennacherib's ground lines are never allowed to assume an identity independent of the figures, and they slant, shift, or terminate to suit the requirements of the figural arrangement" (Russell 1993, 61–62). The style suggests depth and perspective, a "clear attempt to represent pictorial space" and a related "interest in the historically verifiable universe" (Winter 1981, 24). John Russell (1991) also has suggested a genuine connection between the portrayals of scenery and costume and reality in the reliefs of Sennacherib:

> The details that do exist...could...have been drawn wholly from written campaign accounts and interviews with participants from both sides....many inhabitants of captured cities were deported to Assyria, so it should not have been difficult to locate Lachishites to interview...The Lachish shown in the relief is intended to be recognizable. Indeed, its combination of topography, costume, and architectural features is so specific that it seems probable that anyone who had seen the city itself would recognize its image in the reliefs. (1991, 208–209; see also 1993, 64–65)

Through a careful examination of inscriptional material, Russell (1991) provides a list and analysis of those who would have seen the reliefs, providing important information about the purpose of the depictions and the impression to be made by heads and hair. He notes, for example, that in contrast to the written declarations concerning history and the king's power which would have been accessible only to a small literate number of scribally trained Assyrian courtiers, the images

> would have been intelligible to a much broader audience...including foreign visitors, some of whom might have recognized their own people and land in this highly specific image....The image of the fall of Lachish confirms for foreign visitors and subject peoples what they already know—or at least what the Assyrian king wants them to believe—namely, that Assyrian might is invincible....For courtiers, by contrast, these images would have been a pleasant reminiscence of an Assyrian victory as well as a cautionary reminder of the forces at the king' command. (Russell 1991, 256; see also 1993, 72–73)

Russell (1991) describes the audience of the relief, from the perspective of those who planned and executed it: gods, captive workers, foreign visitors, those who bring tribute, the king himself, senior officials, royal attendants, royal scribes, household staff (those who prepare the food, keep house, and serve in various ways), diviners, singers, and various "professionals" who may be foreigners, diplomats, interpreters (238–240). Winter (1981) reminds us that "right from the beginning there was a heterogeneous, ethnic and cultural audience for the palace reliefs" (30) and that as the empire expanded, so did the "prospective audience" for the relief. Indeed, the reliefs provided the diverse members of the Assyrian Empire "a common history" rooted in military events (Winter 1981, 30).

This common history, however, also allowed for portrayals of ethnic difference and identity, partially created by hairstyle. Foreigners visiting or incorporated into palace life would have had to face their subservience with resignation, but would also have been able to find themselves in the picture: their defeated and fallen heroes, their long-suffering wives, their exiled children. The inclusion of Judeans with their own observable ethnic identity, indicated both by costume and head treatment, thus confirmed the power of the Assyrian monarch but also declared the identity and continued existence of Judeans as Judeans. This on-going existence, however, acknowledged their present subjugation and, from the Assyrian perspective, their inferiority. Cifarelli's (1998) criteria of alterity operates in the Lachish reliefs as well.

Drawing comparisons with certain periods in Western culture, Cifarelli (1998) notes that "the exposure of female flesh, even limited exposure of 'innocent' legs and ankles, participates in the signification of availability and immodesty" (220, 221). Women's and girl's hair is consistently portrayed as covered by long head garments that completely enclose the hair and reach down the back (fig. 13). The women and girls in the Lachish reliefs are pictured as deportees on

FIGURE 13. Scene from Lachish relief depicting Judean men and women being marched out of the city (BM 124907, 124908). Copyright Trustees of the British Museum.

the road, so it is possible that these scarflike coverings are outdoors travel head-gear for women. The full, simple covering allows for modesty but is also stripped of the ornamentation connoting possible former wealth or status. A closer ex-amination, however, allows one to see that the women are made to show a bit of ankle and leg and that the front of their garments is shorter than the back. Ci-farelli might suggest that to Assyrian eyes, these representations of the women of Lachish were meant to degrade and demean them. The length of the female Judean refugees' garments becomes more striking when compared with the way in which the garment of the queen of Ashurbanipal reaches to her feet (fig. 14; Barnett 1960, 105; see also Hall 1928, plate XLI 2). This, too, was part of the message conveyed by the reliefs to visitors to the great court of Sennacherib.

The gesture of hairgrasping is found among the reliefs, as an Assyrian sol-dier pulls back on the hair of his enemy, appearing to stab him at the same time (Ussishkin 1982, 87; Barnett et al. 1998, plate 339,). Many enemies portrayed in the reliefs have their hands raised or crouch in the posture of subservience. Others have been stripped naked and are tortured by flaying or are impaled. All are enemies, to be sure, and all have been defeated at Lachish, but are all Judeans?

The heads and hair of the men defeated at Lachish are portrayed in three ways, as noted above: the helmeted defenders with pointed helmet and earflap, the male deportees with head-fitting, wrapped cloth (Wäfler 1975, 53, 65) or perhaps hats made of leather, again with the side flap that covers the ear, and the hatless, curly haired men (fig. 15; see Wäfler 1975, 65–67). Children, male and female, are pictured as smaller sized adults, dressed identically to their elders. The beards of the adult male deportees on the road who carry baggage overhead or walk by the wagon are sometimes incised with lines to connote tex-ture; the style of their hair is difficult to see; some hair may be seen in a clump at the nape of the neck emerging from the helmet, hat, or head-wrap, but it is not clearly demarcated as the relief now exists (see Ussishkin 1982, 86, 87, detail segment 5). Defeated men at Lachish are more commonly portrayed with short, crisp, curls covering the head and face (see fig. 15). These round, sculpted curlicues characterize the hairstyles of dead soldiers in segment 5 (Ussishkin 1982, 86, 87) and of bowing prisoners in segment 6 (Ussishkin 1982, 88, 89), where body language connotes subjugation, petition, and prostration (see also Barnett et al. 1998, plate 329). No fillet holds back the hair, in contrast to typical Bronze Age portrayals. What accounts for these variations—role in the battle, status, ethnicity?

Barnett (1958) believed all the men to be Judeans but to have served dif-ferent functions reflected by their headgear. The warrior defenders of Lachish on the towers wear pointed helmets like their Assyrian counterparts, but the

FIGURE 14. Relief of Ashurbanipal and his queen, from the North Palace of Ashurbanipal (BM 124920). Copyright Trustees of the British Museum.

FIGURE 15. Prisoners from Lachish, wall panel relief (BM 124909). Copyright Trustees of the British Museum.

helmets are distinguished by the side flaps, found also on the headgear of deportees, leaders who are being exiled. Barnett also viewed the curly-haired men without hats as Judeans. They are singled out for special roughness and flaying. In his 1958 essay Barnett suggested that the "men with the peculiar head-dresses are native inhabitants of Lachish," whereas "the men in the long dresses with curly hair who have so incensed Sennacherib must be Hezekiah's men, the Jews who influenced the city to resist" (163). Barnett postulated, in fact, that the Judeans with the flap headdress appear in other reliefs, worn by members of the royal bodyguard in the passage to the Ishtar temple (fig. 16; Barnett et al. 1998, plates 485, 484). On the basis of the flap headgear, Barnett et al. (1998, plate 122) also identified as Judean prisoners working in a quarry from scenes in Sennacherib's temple at Nineveh Court VI (see fig. 17). Judean men with the crisply curled beards and hair may in his view possibly be found among the musicians in room XLVII (fig. 18; Barnett et al. 1998, plate 399; see also Wäfler 1975, 60). The identity of the men with curls at Lachish is debated, however, and with this debate come reminders of the caution with which we must approach artistic renderings of ethnic identity.

Collon (2005), Albenda (1982), and Reade (1999) note that the curled hair and facial features might also be compared with portrayals of Nubians and Egyptians, for example, on the seventh-century BCE wall relief of Ashurbanipal

FIGURE 16. Members of the royal bodyguard, passage to the Ishtar temple (BM 124951). Copyright Trustees of the British Museum.

depicting the siege of an Egyptian city (fig. 19; Barnett 1976, plate XXXVI; Hall 1928, plate XL). J. J. M. Roberts (2006) points to the important political and military roles played by the Egyptians and Nubians in eighth-century BCE Palestine. Judean leaders and those of other nearby cities called upon Egypt to help in their rebellion against Assyrian rule, a resistance in which Egypt was eager to take part (see Isaiah 20:3–5 and Roberts' [2006] interpretation of Isaiah 14:32, 18,30:1–5, and 31:1–3; also 2 Kings 18:19–24). It may thus be possible that Egyptian and/or Nubian troops are depicted by the Assyrians as being at Lachish. The bound prisoners defeated in the war relief of Ashurbanipal appear to have curly hair but no beards. Is it possible that in line with Cifarelli's (1998) discussion of alterity, the Egyptians or Nubians at Lachish were depicted not clean-shaven as they preferred to be, but as hairy barbarians, whereas the refugee Judeans who would have worn beards have only stubble, their beards having been shaved as an act of humiliation? Cifarelli (1998) writes that "distinctive patterns of haircutting and shaving appear to have been used to communicate a

FIGURE 17. Relief of Judean prisoners pulling a rope while working in a quarry. From Sennacherib's temple at Nineveh, Court VI (RSM 1874.7.2). Copyright Trustees of the National Museums of Scotland.

FIGURE 18. Musicians playing lyres, relief from Sennacherib's temple at Nineveh (BM 124974). Copyright Trustees of the British Museum.

FIGURE 19. Assyrian capture of a fortress in Egypt, relief of Ashurbanipal (BM 124928). Copyright Trustees of the British Museum.

man's status or occupation, from the degrading haircuts ordained for prisoners, criminals, and slaves to the ritual shaving used in the consecration of priests" (219; see also Winter 1997, 371). Chapman (2004) points to the image in one of Sennacherib's reliefs of "an Assyrian soldier grasping a prisoner by the beard before he either cuts off his beard or cuts off the prisoner's head with a dagger held in the hand" (39, plate 2; see fig. 20). Was the presence or absence of facial hair on male enemies at Lachish a purposeful comment by Assyrian artists concerning the lowly status of the defeated?

Conclusions

The study of portrayals of hair in ancient Near Eastern art provides interesting visual information that may shed light on the role and significance of hair in ancient Israelite literature. Work with the artistic representations and the material culture of hair underscores critical methodological issues pertaining to the way we see and to the psychological, social, and political dimensions of hair as sign and symbol. Our study points further to the complex relationships between hair and identity in cultural and multicultural settings.

One possible real-life implication of Late Bronze Era Egyptian representations of Philistine hair and of what may be the hair of Israelites is that the generally smooth-shaven appearance of Philistines contrasts with that of bearded, long-haired Israelites. This contrast corresponds with the symbolic, descriptive means by which Israelites distinguish between themselves and the enemy Philistine "Other." The hairstyles of Judean pillar figures from the Iron Era may provide evidence of certain Israelite women's hairstyles in the period of the Judean monarchy, but it is impossible to be certain. Real women's hairstyles may have differed from village to village; different styles may have reflected age or class, and the relationship between conventionalized artistic renditions and the hairstyles of real women cannot be ascertained. Assyrian Iron Age portrayals of men's hair vary, including helmeted warriors and refugees whose hair is enclosed by close-fitting head coverings with side-flaps, the soft-hatted Jehu, whose pointy, perhaps cloth, head covering folds back like a hunter's cap, and the curly-headed warriors, be they Judeans or Nubians/Egyptians, with short hair who wear no hat or fillet, but whose stiff curls ring the head. Again, roles or tastes may be reflected in these differences, and the importance of Assyrian artistic convention needs to be considered, as does the possibility that bearded Nubians or Egyptians and less fully bearded Judeans are purposefully portrayed as the Other, wearing their hair after defeat in battle in some imposed style and not as they themselves would choose to wear it. We have also explored

FIGURE 20. Alabaster wall panel. The march of prisoners, from Sennacherib's southwest palace, Quyunjiq, Room XIV (BM 124786). Copyright Trustees of the British Museum.

the difficulty of identifying ethnic hairstyles in the absence of labeling by the ancient artists. Scholars disagree, for example, about the identity of the men with curly hair and beards at Lachish.

For smooth-shaven Egyptians, the beards of their northern neighbors may have conveyed otherness, an otherness shared by Syrians and Canaanites. For Assyrians whose kings are portrayed with long hair and beards, the shorter hairdos of Judean enemies at Lachish may convey subservience, a decrease in manly status. Is the occasional shaved Syrian prisoner in Egyptian art an image of humiliation, or is this portrayal just an artistic variation or the work of an artist less familiar with conventional portrayals? Judean women's hair is fully covered in Assyrian art, perhaps pointing to the drama of having the woman's hair visible in the ritual for the woman suspected of adultery in Numbers 5.

We have also asked who would have seen these various portrayals of hair. Portrayals propagandize and encapsulate the power of the state for audiences exposed to them, and the hairstyle would contribute to the impression made. In the Assyrian case, scholars suggest that portrayals of foreigners with their different hairstyles and costumes were meant to convey the multiculturalism of the empire and its peoples. Members of these conquered groups, who would have worked as forced labor in the palace, or visited, bearing tribute in a set-ting of diplomacy, may have seen themselves portrayed in the art. The message might have been that they were now subservient to the Assyrian king, but they did have their place in the empire and their own identity as part of that rich diversity. Notions of social body and body politic apply, for they were now not only part of their own cultural group but also belonged to a larger social entity, the peoples of the empire. They were also forced to act their part, to wear their status. Their own sense of identity and ethnicity was affected by others' portray-als of them.

How might Judeans have reacted emotionally and personally to portray-als of their fellows in the Lachish reliefs, to scenes of their forced march with women and children out of the city? Perhaps they recognized the way the wives covered their hair for the journey; perhaps they appreciated having survived. Scenes of the battles, with unmistakable Israelite hair treatment, different from that of their enemies, might have reminded them of those who were lost. Such portrayals might have led to resignation or to hopes of future resistance. The responses might have been varied and complex. But throughout, hair was a critical part of how they were perceived by others and how they were made to perceive themselves. Hair complexly reflects identity as experienced, projected, or imposed. Just as notions of personal body, social body, and body politic lead to questions about artistic representations of Israelite hair, these categories help to understand hair in the Hebrew Bible.

The Hebrew Bible is a major resource for understanding the religion and culture of the ancient Israelites through their own eyes, or at least through the eyes of the various and varied contributors to the biblical tradition. Certain scenes and passages that involve hair come to mind for any reader of the Bible: the hero Samson's unshorn locks, source of his strength, shaved because of Delilah's treachery; the killing of Absalom, rebel son of David, made possible when his long locks catch and suspend him in the branches of a tree; the description of the Nazirite vow in Numbers 6, which involves the temporary assumption of a set-apart, holy status for men or women, who agree not to cut their hair and to avoid drinking wine and contact with the dead, a source of impurity in a priestly worldview; the letting down of the hair of the woman accused of adultery in a ritual description in another priestly passage, Numbers 5; and the shaving of heads of captive women prescribed in Deuteronomy 21, a treatment of those who have become the unhappy spoils of war. These passages and their implications are the focus of four chapters of this book, but other biblical references to hair and related symbols and symbolic actions also come into play as we apply some of the comparative and interdisciplinary approaches explored at the opening of this project. Certain recurring words lead to relevant biblical texts: "hair," "shave," "cut," "razor," "beard," and *pr'*, a difficult-to-translate term that has to do with loose or long hair. An underlying and basic methodology of this study has been to work with the concordance to locate the use of these terms in the Hebrew Bible and then to explore how they are contextualized, the patterns of meaning that emerge at exegetical, operational, and positional levels (Turner 1967). This close work leads to the first area of inquiry, the nexus between maleness, warrior status, and holiness revealed beautifully in tales of Samson in Judges 13–16.

3

Samson

Maleness, Charisma, Warrior Status, and Hair

For most people schooled in Western culture, the equation between hair and the Hebrew Bible immediately calls to mind the hero-judge Samson. Tales of Samson in turn lead to other relevant biblical passages and cultural artifacts that reveal issues pertaining to hair and identity and serve as a testing ground for the application of some of the methodological approaches and questions discussed in chapter 1.

In all of the methodological approaches, context is critical. Context takes a number of forms: narrative context; the historical and cultural context presumed by the story; the possible periods in which the tale was told, written, or held meaningful; the audiences to whom it was addressed; and the kind of literature to which it belongs.

It is very tempting as a biblical scholar to begin by giving the reader some sense of the socio-historical setting presumed for stories about Samson, their biblical context, and their similarities to other biblical and ancient Near Eastern literatures, but to do so is to get ahead of ourselves. Instead, let us explore Judges 13–16 as a story, asking how the narrative as preserved in the biblical version contextualizes hair. Samson is a character who relates to his hair in certain ways; hair operates meaningfully in Judges 13–16 in accordance with certain patterns and expectations.

Narrative Context: Individual, Operational, and Social Body

Samson's hair is of overt importance in Judges chapters 13 and 16, the passages that announce his birth and that describe his downfall and death. That he
wears his hair long is implicit, a presumed part of his demeanor in the many
adventures that come between the beginning and end of his life.

In Judges 13, a barren woman learns from a divine emissary, sent explicitly
to announce good news, that she is to give birth to a son. It is clear that the
child is to be special. The messenger instructs the woman to nourish her body
during the pregnancy in a specific way; she is to avoid wine and strong drink
and is not to eat unclean food. After the child's birth, a razor is never to go
across his head, for the child is to be a *nāzîr* from the womb. The root meaning
of this term suggests that he has some sort of set-apart status. He is, moreover,
to begin to rescue Israel from the hand of the Philistines. The activities of a
warrior are thereby suggested. The passage leads the reader to pay special attention to the hair, which is never to be cut. Only the woman hears this information from her first encounter with the divine messenger (13:5); its absence
from traditional-style recurring references to the encounter and to the special
instructions about the child (13:7, 14) underlines the importance both of the
long hair and of the woman, the bearer, who knows more about the matter than
does her husband. It is interesting that Samson's special status, his Nazirite
identity with its long hair, are involuntary conditions conferred upon him or
demanded by a divine power. Without searching beyond Judges 13–16, it is not
certain that the food and uncleanness rules apply to him.

Chapters 14–15 of Judges do not mention Samson's hair, but they present
a particular kind of daring hero, whose adventures are larger than life. Samson is a loner on the drift who kills a lion with his bare hands (14:6), slays a
thousand men with the jawbone of a donkey (15:15), and carries city gates on
his shoulders (16:3). He cannot be tied down by ropes or subdued by men.
He is unable to form lasting social bonds with women, and the disastrous
and destructive events surrounding his marriage to the Philistine woman of
Timnah read like an advertisement against exogamy. Significantly, throughout these chapters, the writer does not comment on Samson's hair as a source
of his super powers. Samson's mother has been told that he is a Nazir; she
has told his father about this status but not about the instructions concerning hair, although one would assume he eventually notices that his son never
cuts his hair. The Judahites know to treat Samson with kid gloves because of
his explosive power and ask his permission at one point to tie him and give
him over to the Philistine oppressors, from whom he will, of course, break

free at will (15:12–14). Do they know the source of his strength? The Philistines clearly do not.

The central theme of Judges chapter 16 is the uncovering of the secret of Samson's immense strength, his uncut hair, through the betrayal of Samson by his lover Delilah, "a woman he loves." The biblical writer thus places the sign of Nazirite status in terms of a traditional folk motif: the hidden source of hero's strength or invincibility. Like so many folk heroes, his strength resides in some feature of his body or clothing or the sword he carries. This magical source of strength, of course, is also the source of his downfall, for to conquer him enemies need only uncover the hidden source. Betrayal by lovers or friends also frequently accompanies the motif of hidden strength. Samson reveals the truth about his hair slowly.

Some suggest that Samson is a fool for love, revealing the truth to Delilah even after she has called the Philistines down upon him three times when he has fed her false answers. Why does Samson not catch on to her plan to betray him? Within traditional literature, such repetitions create emphasis and message. The message is not that Samson is a dolt, but, as Robert Alter (1990) has suggested, that he is addicted to taking chances. One might suggest that he suffers from the common malaise of heroes: hubris. When he has finally "told her his heart" and she has shaved his head, he thinks mistakenly that this revelation will cause no more harm than the others, that the loss of his hair will not affect his strength. "He did not know that God had left him" (16:20).

The repetition in the tales, Delilah's begging for the truth, her accusing Samson of not loving her, and his revelation (false three times and then finally true) follow an interesting pattern that relates to qualities of hair and builds in the direction of the truth about its power in Samson. The first two false responses have to do with strings or threads that bind: tying with rawhide ropes and then binding with rope made of plant material that is twisted and wound. The third response comes closer to the truth and closer to the hair, but also suggests the image of ropes and binding. If the seven plaits of his head are "woven with the loom-stuff" (16:13), he will become weak. For the first time, we hear that Samson wears his long hair not loose, but in plaits, a word rooted in a verb meaning "to pass through." The hair is braided, prepared in a special way implying care, working with the hair, a particular style, and a degree of control—in short, a culture of hair. A man's woven hair is plaited and then bound up in a woman's weaving on the loom. Samson's hair is woven like the cloth of the loom to which the false revelation alludes. Even weaving the hair does not weaken him, but when the seven plaits are removed by shaving, Samson does become weak like other men. The Philistines gouge out his eyes and, blind and bald, he becomes defenseless and infantile. His enemies bring him forth to play before them like a dancing bear. But his hair has grown back! Foolish Philistines. With the hair, now wild, loose, and free, comes superhuman strength, and Samson brings down a building upon his celebrating enemies.

What can be learned from the narrative context in tales of Samson? Samson himself knows that his hair is a source of strength and that he has been a Nazir, set aside since the womb, and yet he dares to forgo the hair, not fully accepting that divine power is what empowers him and that it resides somehow in the hair. Hair operates in the narratives to make Samson a tragic hero who suffers a downfall; he experiences an apotheosis when the hair grows back. Within the story, hair is thus related to a kind of life force, connoting a heroic status that sets Samson apart from other people. The significance of the hair is a secret, at least to the Philistines, and they do not pay adequate respect to the power contained in it. The deportment of the hair, in fact, parallels the stages in Samson's life as a hero: the superhuman strength of the seven-plaited hero who lets loose his incredible power when needed, the impotence of the shaven hero betrayed by his lover, and the liberated, exploding, uncontrollable strength of the hero with wild, unbound, newly grown hair who kills all his enemies with himself. Samson's hair introduces to his tales important contrasts between "the raw and the cooked," as Claude Lévi-Strauss has described the contrast between nature and culture.

Samson's hairdo as plaited is culturally intensive, although in many ways he is a creature of the wild, living in caves, using weapons from nature, and unable to form stable relationships with anyone but his parents. This play between nature and culture, freedom and control, is important in understanding Samson. He explodes in violence, untamed, like a volcano, but he speaks in riddles and proverbs and engages in clever trickery. His hairstyle is culturally intensive even while being long and natural in the sense that it is untouched by the technology of cutting. It thus contains the very qualities of betwixt-and-between identity typical of this charismatic hero, who moves between the cave and the town, the Israelites and the Philistines, and who hovers on the border of animal and human, human and divine.

The hair that makes Samson a superman also renders him marginal and vulnerable; the woman who shaves his hair tames him. The third repetition of the exchange between Samson and Delilah concerning the source of his strength is critical to this gendered tug of war and reveals much about hair, the social body, and a particular culture, even within the contours of one scene. To allow someone access to one's hair is to allow a degree of intimacy, to express trust, for hair, like any part of the body, is an extension of the person himself. To allow Delilah to weave his hair into her loom is to allow her to make him a part of her domestic activity, part of her own creative work as a weaver. Samson thus flirts with danger, and actions involving his hair suggest vulnerability even before the true revelation. As Bal (1984) has observed, to reveal the full truth that inevitably leads to the shaving of his head is a complete surrender of the hero to the heroine, Israelite to Philistine. Delilah the woman now has taken power over the man whose strength resides in his hair. Samson's "body politics" of hair within the tale cycle involve the imposition of hair shaving upon him and his loss of power and autonomy. One thinks back to the Manchu's imposition of the queue on the Han Chinese. One also thinks of Berg's (1951) Freudian-based suggestions about the link between castration and hair cutting. Cut hair does not connote castration in a universal sense. In the context of this tale, which plays upon the relationship between Samson and Delilah and the role of hair within the relationship, however, the woman's shaving of the hero does suggest his unmanning.

Within its narrative context, hair is thus involved in complex shifts in gender relations and in negotiating difficult political and social relations between Israelites and their dominant, oppressive Philistine neighbors. Samson's hair demarcates a border where nature and culture overlap and declares his "set aside" status as a Nazir, involving special birth, divine election, and possibly other circumscribed relations to food and drink. To tend or cut another's hair is to have power over them, to be intimately involved with them. Hair is identity and loss of hair is loss of identity. For Samson, hair is related to strength, dominance as a man, and the activities of a warrior.

To move beyond the boundaries of the tale itself in exploring a trajectory of hair meanings requires a broader positional analysis beginning with background information concerning the socio-historical setting of the tales and relevant examples of material culture. Against this background, we can then trace paths suggested by key terms and features of the narratives about Samson as understood within the broader context of the Hebrew Bible.

Historical Cultural Setting

Within the biblical chronology, the Samson narrative is set in premonarchic times, in the days of the so-called judges, charismatic temporary and nondynastic leaders who arise among the people because of their military prowess and due to perceptions that they are somehow touched by God. Many of the biblical judges are unusual leaders in some respect, left-handed like Ehud in a symbolic universe in which the left is the sneaky and untrustworthy side, female like Deborah in a world in which political power belongs to men, an exiled illegitimate son like Jephthah born to a culture in which the eldest legitimate son inherits the patrimony. They are marginal figures in tales of self-definition that Steven Weitzman (2002) has described as "border fiction." They are portrayed as "social bandits" in terms employed by the social historian Eric Hobsbawm (1981). Like the British social bandit Robin Hood, the judges fight those who wield power over them, often using the underdogs' weapons of deception and trickery to liberate their people. Samson is one of these border figures, and marginal, betwixt-and-between qualities are related to his hair. He is an explosive sort of social bandit whom Hobsbawm dubs "the avenger."

A first question concerning the beautifully crafted biblical setting for tales of Samson that paint a particular picture of premonarchic Israel, its form of polity, and the problems of its people, is whether tales of Samson find some historical verisimilitude in actual premonarchic times, that is in Iron Age I, the period that roughly spans the twelfth to the end of the eleventh centuries BCE. Many scholars agree that tales of Samson do reflect an early Iron Age setting quite well, for central to the tales and to our study of hair in the story of Samson is the competition between Israelites and Philistines for land and hegemony in the area to the east of the Mediterranean coast that once may have been home to the Danites, the tribe of Samson.

Philistines, Identity, and Hair

The Philistines were one of several Sea Peoples who migrated from their home-lands in the Aegean to settle on the southeast coast of the Mediterranean in the early twelfth century BCE. They continued to control the coastal area for the next 600 years, and their major cities Ashdod, Ashkelon, Ekron, Gaza, and Gath all figure in biblical narratives. Archaeological evidence clearly identifies and distinguishes this group both from the Israelites and from other contemporary Canaanite neighbors in terms of building design, food preferences, pottery style, clothing, and hair customs (see Bloch-Smith 2003, 412–425; Stager 1998, 153, 159–165). Iron Age I Philistine pottery shared much in design with Mycenaean material, with its decorative painted creatures (e.g., birds and feather helmeted warriors) and complex painted geometric shapes. In contrast, Israelite/Canaanite pottery was much plainer. The Philistines raised hogs and ate pork, the bones of which have not been found in Israelite/Canaanite sites. Moreover, as indicated by the study of artistic representations (see chapter 2), if the dominant scholarly identifications are correct, Philistines are portrayed in Near Eastern art of the period as clean shaven, whereas Israelites and neigh-boring peoples, such as the Syrians, have beards. Philistines wear feathered or spiked headdresses when portrayed as participants in war or as prisoners of war, and their hair seems not to be a visible feature of their presentation as warriors. Israelite warriors, however, have shoulder-length hair, held in place by a fillet, and beards (contrast figs. 4 and 7).

It is clear that the Israelites considered the Philistines to be uncircumcised, but concerning this important bodily signifier we have no extrabiblical evidence. Indeed, certain other Sea Peoples are said to be circumcised in an important Egyptian source, the Great Karnak inscription of the pharaoh Merneptah (see Machinist 2000, 76, n. 99; 77, n. 101). Lawrence Stager (1998) suggests that the Samson account may reflect a genuine Iron Age I situation in which Israelites and Philistines "interact along the boundaries shared by two distinctive cultures, Semitic and early Greek" (154). In the mid-eleventh century BCE, the Philistines expanded into the highland region of the Israelites, leading to serious confrontation and war. The Israelite king David successfully repelled the Philistines, who retreated to the coastal areas by the mid-tenth century BCE. The Philistine presence on the coast continued, however, as did their interactions with Israelites.

Philistine locales and a major city, Ashdod, are mentioned in later biblical sources that allude to conflict and tensions (see, e.g., 1 Kings 15:27, 16: 15–17; 2 Kings 18:8; Amos 1:6–8; Jeremiah 25:20; Zephaniah 2:4–7; Joel 4:4–8; Nehemiah 4:1; 13:23–24; Machinist 2000). Machinist (2000) writes, "Philistines are not simply memories from an older tradition but [are] still existent, in some historical form, through the post-exilic period of Achaemenid Persian domination" (57). The Philistines would have been a historically appropriate enemy for the premonarchic setting of Samson's life, but Philistines also would have been understood as potential enemies by audiences in subsequent renderings of the Samson story, during the monarchy and beyond. Machinist suggests, however, that Philistines retained identity as a quintessential "Other" not because of later disputes, but precisely because of their antagonistic presence in the land at the time "when Israel became an organized society" (69) (i.e., genuinely early in Israel's history). What about the significance of hair?

Philistines are portrayed in art as less hairy than Israelites and certainly less hairy than the Nazir Samson. Hair thus becomes an important way in which the Israelite author reflects upon Israelite identity and culturally demarcates his people from the uncircumcised Other. That the enemy is Philistine makes Samson's never cutting his hair especially important. It marks both cultural difference and the attempt to impose one's culture on the other. Israelite writers and audiences who identify with the story cycle are implicitly suggesting that the Israelite hero's hairiness is not only better than Philistine smoothness but that it is related to his greater strength. Philistines are portrayed as trying to rid themselves of the hero's hairiness and thereby to assert that their own culture is dominant. The Israelite response, through the story as related, implicitly is, "You are too stupid even to notice or worry when the powerful, symbolically loaded hair grows back." Hair is cultural identity to an exponential degree in the case of an Israelite Nazir engaged in conflict with Philistines, for his hair has never been cut. The ways in which Delilah and the Philistines react to and interact with Samson's hair, first ignoring its implications, then, after hearing Samson's revelations, weaving it, womanizing it, and shaving it, suggest that they attempt to devalue it and yet are afraid of it. This is very much the way bordering ethnic cultures react to one another, in deprecation, distrust, fear, and aggression (Thomas 2006).

In exploring the context of hair in the Samson story cycle in a socio-historical sense, it is important to consider the meanings of the tales to Israelites in different socio-historical settings. The ways in which Samson's hair was understood may have evolved. It makes a difference whether Philistines really were competing with Israelites when the story was told. Did they become a "symbol" for the enemy rather than the enemy itself? Do we know how Philistines or Israelites wore their hair, for example, in the time of Joel, a postexilic prophet? Would the hair motif have held meaning later in Israelite history to demarcate ethnic differences, or did it become an internal Israelite issue, a matter of ritual status? To delve more deeply into our contextual analysis, we now turn to key terms and where they lead in the traditions of the Hebrew Bible.

Biblical Context: The Term Nazir

Central to an understanding of hair in tales of Samson is the term *nāzîr* and notions attached to it. The term is rooted in the verb meaning "separate." In a negative sense, Isaiah 1:4 and Ezekiel 14:5, 7 describe the sinful people as literally "separating back" (i.e., being estranged from God). More often, the root connotes the sense of consecration or dedication. Leviticus 22:2 describes donations that are holy to God as "set apart." The priests' role is to "separate the people from their uncleanness" (Leviticus 15:31). With intense irony, the prophet Hosea denounces the people's sinfulness by saying that they have separated or "consecrated themselves to shame" in worshiping Baal, the Canaanite deity (Hosea 9:10).

Many of the terms derived from *nzr*, however, refer to symbols or signs of a set apart, consecrated, special status involving the hair, head, or headdress, all of which are related. In the Hebrew Bible, a common noun derived from the root is *nezer*, a term that seems to mean a crown or the condition of being royalty of some sort. The Amalekite who claims to have killed Saul, when the king asked to be put out of his wounded misery, brings David, the would-be king, Saul's crown, his *nezer,* as evidence he is dead. The *nezer* is a symbol of the man who was formerly "set apart" by God (see also 2 Kings 11:12; 2 Chronicles 23:11; Proverbs 27:24; Psalms 89:40; 132:18). The set-aside status is also applied to Joseph in formulaic language found in the ancient poems at Genesis 49:26 and Deuteronomy 33:16: *ûlĕqodqōd nĕzîr 'eḥāyw,* literally "for the head of the one who is set apart from his brothers" (see also Lamentations 4:7, where the term perhaps means "princes" or royalty; those set apart). Leviticus 21:12 refers to the special status of the priest who is "exalted above his follows" because of "the consecration" of the anointing of oil poured on his head. Again, setting apart, holiness, and special consecrated status have to do with the head. Similarly, what appears to be a special gem often translated "diadem" is called a *nēzer* and is worn in some sort of turban or headdress of the priest (Exodus 29:6; 39:30; see also Zechariah 9:16).

The Nazir, Samson, like others so designated in the Hebrew Bible, is also one who is separate, consecrated, and devoted in some sense and whose status clearly has symbolism related to the head. In addition to the hair is a related complex of symbols pertaining to Nazirism to be explored in cultural and literary-biblical contexts.

In Judges 13–16, Samson's status as a Nazir is related to his pregnant mother's abstinence from fermented products of the grapevine, her avoidance of food that is unclean, and the promise never to let a razor come across his head, a promise he keeps for his entire life until Delilah intervenes. The larger biblical context (e.g., Numbers 6:3–4 and Amos 2:11–12) suggests that the avoidance of wine, in particular, is always a part of what one might call the ritual condition of the Nazir, even though differences emerge in the understanding of this ritual condition, in particular between Numbers 6 and other references, a matter to be explored in detail in chapter 4. Wine and hair are part of a shared symbolic complex.

The Social Context of Symbols of Samson's Nazirite Status, Other Than Hair

The wine and the unclean food have to be understood in a wider context to appreciate the cultural resonances of Nazirite status of which uncut hair is a part. We begin with wine. On the one hand, wine is frequently positively or neutrally associated with the daily, the convivial, and the social. Whether practicing hospitality among friends or hoping to appease an enemy, people are often pictured bringing or sharing wine. Hannah gives wine and other comestibles to Eli, the priest, when she brings her son Samuel to serve him. Similarly, Jesse, father of David, sends wine to Saul, the anointed leader, by means of David. Abigail sets wine before David in his bandit phase as a sign of welcome and appeasement, lest he strike out against her inhospitable husband and his household (1 Samuel 25:18). People are frequently described transporting wine (1 Samuel 10:3), a product of the agrarian economy which is appreciated by human beings, a sign of the land's bounty and divine blessing. Wine is also a ritual means of communion in the daily drink offering (Exodus 29:40; Leviticus 23:13; see also the intriguing scene between Abraham and Melkizedek in Genesis 14:18). Together with bread, wine connotes social participation in the meal, with frequent implications of joy, sharing, and gladness (Isaiah 22:13; Judges 9:13). Wine is, moreover, a cultural medium; it must be fermented and requires skill in production. Thus, after Enkidu, the hairy wild man of the Mesopotamian Gilgamesh epic, is socialized through a sexual encounter with a courtesan, he partakes of bread and "strong drink." On one level, then, to abstain from wine is to be removed from the social and the cultural.

On the other hand, wine in Hebrew Bible is also associated with excess and antisocial behavior, as in the cases of the drunken Lot (Genesis 19:32–35) who sires children with his own daughters, and Noah (9:21), who exposes his nakedness to his sons (see also 2 Samuel 13:28 and Genesis 27:25). To drink wine is to lose control or to throw over one's proper responsibilities (Isaiah 5:11, 22; 28:1; Amos 2:8). An interesting thread in Hebrew Bible thus requires abstinence—for example, on the part of priests who serve in the sanctuary (Leviticus 10:8–10; Ezekiel 44:21). In Leviticus 10, an implicit parallel is drawn between abstaining from wine and drinking it, holiness and the everyday or mundane, and the pure or clean and the unclean. Thus, to not drink wine is to be set apart both from normal social activity and from the excesses to which humans are drawn. In some trajectories in ancient Israelite culture, to abstain from wine is to partake of the holy and the sacred, to be ritually available to the deity and identified with the divine. The proscription concerning drinking wine for the Nazir in this way parallels the proscription concerning food. He is to eat no unclean food in accordance with some version of the list detailed in the priestly passage Leviticus 11.

Of great relevance to the drinking habits of the Nazir is the description in Jeremiah 35 of a group called the Rechabites whose ancestor hero forbids them not only to imbibe wine, but also to live in houses, to sow seed, or to plant vineyards; instead, they live in tents. The image, on one level, is of abstinence, and Jeremiah seems to admire the self-discipline of the Rechabites who keep the vow to hold to this regime, in contrast with Israelites, who do not obey the commands of God. Again, however, the group of related symbols suggests a certain kind of nonsocialized stance, a counter-cultural way of life in which people eschew the sharing of wine, living in houses, and agricultural activity. It is as if they are returning to a preagricultural, nomadic form of existence. To be sure, such an existence has its own culture and social world, and, as Elizabeth Grosz (1994) has suggested in regard to symbols of the body, we should not expect simple dichotomies between nature and culture. Nevertheless, the Rechabites seem to adopt a way of life that has less permanent effect on the natural landscape. In a comparable way, the Nazir allows the hair to grow, untreated by man-made instruments, and a term derived from Nazir refers to an uncut vine which is left in its natural state, like the uncut hair of Samson the Nazir. The vines are to be untouched during special divinely demarcated times, namely the seven-year sabbatical and fifty-year jubilee when the land is to lie fallow and is given rest, when debts are forgiven, and slaves are freed (Leviticus 25:5, 11). The time during which the vines are left uncut implies the overturning of normal workaday social structure and hierarchies, a time to let things be.

The Nazir is thus a special kind of demarcated person, set apart, holy, and self-disciplined in adhering to these rules; he is counter-cultural. Not drinking wine keeps him socially removed from an important manufactured agricultural product that forms relationships between people and between humans and God. While Rechabites are not Nazirites, nevertheless one sees some of the same nuances in the symbol systems that surround them. We do not know why the propounder of the rules, Jonadab of Rechab, calls upon his descendants to obey such customs of abstinence or what inspires him; Samson, however, is a Nazir as commanded by the deity through his emissary in an annunciation to his mother. The status is thus involuntary. In this respect, Samson's being a Nazir also sharply contrasts with the description of the voluntary Nazirite vow in Numbers 6. We will set Numbers 6 aside for the moment because it provides important evidence concerning the direction in which views of Nazirism and hair develop, a matter to which we will turn in the next chapter. Samson can be directly compared with other biblical figures and leads to a wider examination of men's long hair in context. A nexus emerges shared by hairiness, maleness, unusual birth and/or divine selection and by hair, warrior status, and leadership.

Samuel and Related Evidence

Like Samson's mother, Hannah, the mother of Samuel, is a barren woman. Her story is told with consummate pathos. Her husband loves her, but her co-wife makes her feel a lesser and unfulfilled woman in the culture to which they belong (1 Samuel 1:6). In this setting, women of child-bearing age are expected to be married and to give birth, continuing male lines. In the scene in 1 Samuel 1, Hannah pours out her heart to the priest Eli, who serves at the sanctuary of Shiloh, where her extended family has come to offer a yearly sacrifice. No divine emissary appears to tell Hannah about her future son, but Hannah herself offers a vow. If God grants her "a seed of men/humans" then she "will give him to God for all the days of his life, and a razor will not go up on his head" (1 Samuel 1:11).

The formulaic language concerning the razor invokes Judges 13:5 and its Nazirite implications, although the term Nazir is not used in the Masoetic version of the tale. The fuller manuscript traditions from Qumran and the Septuagint more fully share the language of Judges 13:15, mentioning the Nazirite status of the boy to be born, his avoidance of wine and strong drink, and his never using a razor (see 1 Samuel 1:11 LXX[B] and 4QSamuel[a]). The Qumran version of 1 Samuel 1:22 also explicitly mentions Samuel's becoming a Nazir forever (see the text-critical discussion by McCarter 1980, 53–54; 56–57). It has been suggested that the preservers or translators of the Samuel material copied from tales of Samson, but, rather than think in terms of literal borrowing, we do well to think in terms of cultural expectations. The son of a barren woman who becomes a great leader, who has special connections to the deity, and who is never to cut his hair is a Nazir, whether the term is used or not. The use of the more extended formulaic descriptions and the specific reference to the Nazir in some versions is to be expected. He is one set apart from birth. That some implications of Nazirite status in Israelite tradition were generally understood and recognized is confirmed by an interesting text in Amos 2:10–11.

The eighth-century BCE prophet Amos describes Israel's lack of covenant faithfulness. He relates the founding myth by which Yhwh rescued the Israelites in Egypt, nourished them in the wilderness wanderings, and gave them the land, allowing them to disinherit its earlier inhabitants. One of the ways in which Amos points to the people's qualities as ingrate involves the Nazirites. In the voice of God Amos declares,

> And I raised up some from among you to be prophets,
> and some from your young men to be Nazirites.
> Is not this true, Israelites? says the Lord.
> But you made the Nazirites drink wine,
> and against the prophets, you commanded, saying,
> "Do not prophesy."

The Nazir is set in parallelism with the prophet. Like the prophet, the Nazir has been "raised up" by God himself, a special charismatic in the community. The Nazir here, as in Judges 13, 1 Samuel 1:11 (in the versions preserved in the

Septuagint and at Qumran), and Numbers 6 is to abstain from wine. The term "young man," *bāḥûr*, moreover, suggests youth and virility. So the young Saul is described in one of the passages favorable to him (1 Samuel 9:2). Amos here imagines Nazirism to be an ancient and sacred institution. As in the cases of Samson and Samuel, the status is involuntary; the Nazir is singled out and special.

Another aspect of Samson and Samuel's Nazirite status involves war. Samuel acts as a prophet who knows God's will; he anoints kings as God commands and is able to predict the future. He is also described as a kind of circuit judge who travels the land to adjudicate disputes, but his role, like that of the judge Deborah, is also closely related to matters of war. Barak, a great warrior, refuses to go to battle without Deborah at his side because she has the connection to God that allows for victory (Judges 4:8–9). Similarly, Samuel gathers Israel before battle at Mizpah, offers sacrifice, gains divine support, and thus assures the success of Israel in battle.

Chosenness, maleness, martial associations, unusual birth, and certain bodily treatments, most visibly long hair, all relate to Nazirite status. When seeking the meanings of hair in ancient Israel, it is also important to explore cases when a number of these characteristics coalesce in biblical portrayals even when Nazirite status is not specifically mentioned. In this way, we see how the biblical writers portray characters to think about the meaning and implications of hair. Even minus mention of Nazirite status per se, hairiness, maleness, war, and charisma share the same web of connotations. The positional analysis thus continues.

Judges 5:2 and Deuteronomy 32:42 include the difficult to translate word *pr`*, which has been variously understood by both modern and ancient interpreters. This term is frequently found in the context of hair and the head and is relevant to the associations explored above among holiness, charisma, and martial ability. In some contexts, the term *pr`* clearly refers to long hair that has not been cut, for example, in the case of Numbers 6, that describes instructions for a temporary version of Nazirite status. Similarly, hair described using this root may be disheveled and/or freely flowing, as in descriptions of people who "wear" the state of mourning or of others who display a state of uncleanness due to leprosy (explored in chapter 5). Most literally, the root *pr`* means "let go, let loose" (Brown et al 1968 828 III [hereafter cited as BDB]). Soggin (1981) moves from "let go" to "burst forth" or "liberate" and translates Judges 5:2, the phrase that opens an ancient, perhaps twelfth century BCE, victory hymn, "Because in Israel the people have regained liberty" (84). Boling (1975), working somewhat more closely with the root meaning and influenced perhaps by biblical usages that refer to free, unbound, or disheveled hair, translates the line in Judges 5:2,

"When they cast off restraint in Israel" (107), although he expresses sympathy for Craigie's translation, "When in Israel men were dedicated unconditionally." Craigie links *pr*ʿ with the Arabic *faraga,* "used in the sense of volunteering for war" (1968, 399). In this way, the first colon of Judges 5:2 parallels the second that describes Israel "presenting themselves" for war (see Rabin 1955; Exodus 35:29, 36:3; Leviticus 22:18; Numbers 15:3). To present for war is to become a free-will offering in a sacrificial sense. Again, in the light of Samson's long hair, which is a sign of dedication to God, and Numbers 6, in which the hair is actually offered up on the altar at the termination of the temporary vow of dedication, the translation of *pr*ʿ as referring to hair seems to make sense.

In a creative reading, Janzen (1989) pays special attention to biblical usages of *pr*ʿ that do not deal specifically with hair and concludes that the "liberation" implicit in the root has to do with "rebellion against structures and constraints claimed (rightly or wrongly) to be foundational to true life giving order" (403–404) He translates, "When rebels cast off restraint in Israel" (405) and sets the line in a socio-historical context of rebellion against oppressors.

Relating the Hebrew to Arabic terms meaning "overtop," "excel," and "noble, eminent man," BDB (328 I) suggests "For the leading of leaders (in Israel)." Based on a Ugaritic text in which the root *pr*ʿ seems to be used ordinally in reference to amounts of wine, Coogan (1978) translates, "In the very beginning in Israel" (145). Cyrus Gordon (1965) also directs the reader to a postbiblical Hebrew *lmpr*ʿ, "at the beginning" (see *Ugaritic Textbook* [UT] 1086.1; also UT 471, no. 2113); yet Rabbinic usages of *pr*ʿ generally have to do with wild hair. A few uses of *pr*ʿ in number contexts seem to refer to a numerical list that is disrupted, "out of order" or "counting backward," "disarranged' as Jastrow (1950) puts it. The list of numbers is thus "disheveled" and fits the root etymology "let loose" best.

Support for hair-related translations of the term *pr*ʿ is found in Deuteronomy 32:42, although here too translation is difficult. In a divine warrior context, the deity Yahweh, Anat-like, speaks of his victory.

> I will make my arrows drunk with blood.
> My sword will devour flesh
> from the blood of the wounded and captive
> from the wild-haired enemy.

The last colon says literally "from the head of the *pĕrāʿôt* of the enemy." The term is the seeming plural feminine noun based on the root *pr*ʿ, found in Judges 5:2. As in the case of Judges 5:2, some would locate the etymology in the notion of primacy or high status (BDB 328 I) and translate "from the head of the leaders of the enemy." There are, however, many places in scripture in which the head is used metonymically to refer to hair, as in Numbers 6:9 "He contaminated (literally) the head of his Nazirite status" and in which the head and the root pr` refer to locks of hair in a lengthy, unbound, or disheveled state. A most pertinent passage is Numbers 6:5 pertaining to the Nazir: "holy he shall be, growing long the pr` of the hair of his head." The New Revised Standard Version translates pera` "locks" as a kind of collective noun. Similarly, in reference to the Levites, sons of Zadok, Ezekiel 44:20 reads, "Their heads they shall not shave, and the pera` they shall not (literally) 'shoot forth,' (that is 'send forth,' 'grow long,' or 'let down'). They shall by all means trim their (literally) heads." As in Numbers 6:9, the head often stands for the hair. See also Numbers 5:18, in which the priest unbinds the hair of the woman accused of adultery: "And he will pr` the head of the woman." In Numbers 6, pr` serves as a verb for the act of letting hair loose rather than the loose, free, long hair itself, and again the head refers to the hair.

Taken as a group these various passages do seem to support a hair-related interpretation of pr` with the accompanying implication for Judges 5:2 and Deuteronomy 32:42 that in ancient Israel, as elsewhere in the wider ancient Near Eastern and Mediterranean world, the young warrior was frequently pictured as wild haired or long haired, the hair possibly relating to his warrior's prowess and power.

Absalom

David's son Absalom is singled out among royal princes for his hair. Hair is important to the characterization drawn by the biblical writer and to the description of Absalom's downfall. The biblical writer plays upon the motif of hair because of its rich connotations within the culture. Hair is integral to Absalom's role as would-be hero and king, as reflected in his own treatment of his hair and others' reactions to it.

Absalom, the third of David's sons born in Hebron, first emerges as a heroic figure in the tale of his sister, Tamar, who has been raped by their half-brother, Amnon. While David the king barely responds when he hears about the ruin of his daughter and the crime of Amnon, who is portrayed as particularly narcissistic and dastardly in his treatment of the young woman, her brother Absalom nobly takes her under his protection. One sees, in a similar way, the brothers of Dinah reacting to her rape with action while her father Jacob hesitates. Reflected are perhaps the close kinship bonds between the children of the same wife in polygynous households where various tensions and alliances arise and also an assumption that the brother is the manly protector of the sister when the paternal role is neglected. A woman's sexuality belongs to the men around her and is theirs to exchange. We recall Laban's role in giving his sister Rebecca to the emissary of her kinfolk for marriage to Isaac. Men who help themselves to a woman's womb without the approval of her kinsmen are in contempt of social mores and subject to severe treatment. They have not honored their counterparts in a culture in which men's relationships play out around various issues involving honor and shame. While the brothers of Dinah use trickery to take immediate vengeance, Absalom bides his time (2 Samuel 13:23). Two years after his sister was raped, Absalom has his servants kill Amnon during the sheep shearing, a festive event which all the royal sons have attended at Absalom's urging of his father the king. Vengeance has been exacted. The biblical writer may display some ambivalence concerning the rightness of Absalom's vengeance. The modern reader cannot but sympathize with his cause (2 Samuel 13:22; 32–33) as do David's general, Joab, and Absalom's cousin, Jonadab, in one thread of the narrative. In contrast, a thinly veiled description of the event in a mashal or parable by the woman of Tekoa may suggest similarity with Cain's murder of Abel, for Cain and Amnon are both killed in "open country." The implicit comparison between the deeds of Cain and Absalom are surely not a positive assessment of the young man's deed. We know, moreover, that Amnon was the first born of David, the first in line to the throne (2 Samuel 3:2) that the charismatic Absalom covets. Now the rival has been eliminated, but Absalom must flee his father's wrath. Later, he is rehabilitated and welcomed back, only to try to overthrow the aging king himself. Absalom is another of the Bible's ambivalent characters—bold, treacherous, ambitious, charismatic, and jealous of his honor. He is also portrayed as endowed with lots of hair and as interested in his own hair. He is surely no Nazir, but the hair is part of his allure and his charisma and he cultivates it because Israelites associate hair with the qualities of special status, divine selection, maleness, and success in battle that are associated with the Nazir.

As a kind of narrative prelude to the tale of Absalom's attempted usurpation of his father's throne, Hebrew scriptures offers what for biblical writers is an unusually expansive description of the way he looks.

> And compared to Absalom, there was no man as handsome
> in all of Israel, to be praised so much.
> From the sole of his foot to the crown of his head,
> there was not in him a blemish.
> And when he shaved his head—at the end of a year's days,
> he would shave it because it was heavy upon him,
> so he shaved it—

and he weighed the hairs of his head:
two hundred shekels by the king's weight!
(2 Samuel 14:25–26)

Certain images invoke the Nazir, others not. Growing the hair until it is long suggests Nazirite status such as that of Samson or Samuel; the mention of growing the hair for a considerable length of time and then shaving it suggests language concerning the Nazir in Numbers 6, who assumes a voluntary Nazirite status for a specified time and then shaves off the hair and sacrifices it. Absalom shaves his hair, however, not because of the end of a vow, nor has he been chosen to be a permanent Nazir since birth, a man who has never cut his hair. His hair is associated with beauty, with lacking blemish, and the shaving is undertaken because the hair has become too heavy and uncomfortable. A part of Absalom's hair growing/cutting ritual, moreover, is to weigh his own hair to see just how much of it there was. Why grow the hair if it is so cumbersome and why weigh it? Why does the biblical writer describe in such detail both the hair and its being cut? On the one hand, he may be portraying Absalom as a dandy, a narcissist, who is not worthy of kingship. On the other hand, it seems clear that Absalom is portrayed as trying to project a certain image with his hair. The long-haired man is special. It is no coincidence that this description is followed by the mention of his offspring (the beautiful daughter is named Tamar, like his sister). The long hair is clearly associated with fertility and manly fecundity. The author may be suggesting that long hair is evocative enough in ancient Israelite culture that the man whose hair is luxuriantly thick and long is regarded as set apart, like a natural Nazir. He looks as if he is meant to lead and as if God's blessing is on his head. He will be an excellent warrior. The richness of the story, however, lies in the fact that these expectations prove to be wrong. The long hair becomes Absalom's undoing. The author is able to play on this irony, however, only because of cultural associations with hair. The author's account beautifully suggests Obeyesekere's (1981) feedback loop. Human beings' deep-seeded, psychoanalytical notions about hair and sexual power intertwine with the personal characteristics of Absalom, who is a destructively ambitious would-be leader, and with cultural expectations and assumptions about hair.

Absalom displays his cunning and charisma in wooing individual Israelites at the city gate of Jerusalem, the center of polity in the capital, with promises that he would rule cases in their favor were he in power. Like bandits before him, he gathers men around him, but the mention of acquiring a chariot and horses and the men's running ahead of him also seems to imply a showy, propagandistic element in his campaign for his own advancement. He "kisses" all who "do him obeisance" and "steals their heart" (2 Samuel 15:5, 6). He is adept at projecting an image of power, an image to which the hair contributes. The forces of Absalom, who eventually overtly and militarily rebel against David, are defeated by the forces of David, but Absalom himself meets his end when his long hair becomes entangled in the branches of an oak as he rides under it on his mule. That Absalom wears his hair flowing and free is itself a hubristic act and shows him as unable to resist making a show of his hair. Even the wild Samson plaits his hair, and pictorial evidence from the Iron Age portrays Israelite warriors with hair tied by fillets. The warrior who leaves his hair wild and free in battle settings surely courts danger. The text literally says that "his head was held fast in the oak." "Head" is a frequent equivalent to hair, as discussed above.

There is irony in the image of a hanging Absalom and the language used to convey it. The mule is a sign of opulence and kingly power (cf. 1 Kings 1:33, 38, 44). The term for the thicket of the tree is rooted in the meaning "insert/interweave." It is very much like the thick hair of Absalom. In late Hebrew, another term derived from the root means "hairnet." The oak often has sacred connotations, as in the oak of Deborah and a variety of sacred groves mentioned in Hebrew Bible (Judges 4:5; 6:11; Genesis 35:4). Thus Absalom is hoisted by his own petard. His pretensions of being specially selected suggested by the hair, the mule, and the oak lead to his own destruction as hair, and hairlike features of the oak intertwine to capture him and leave him vulnerable and hanging. Indeed, like some of the ancient Greek heroes and heroines, he almost becomes one with the tree, for Joab takes three spears or shafts and thrusts him through the heart while he was still alive in the heart of the tree (2 Samuel 18:14). An equation is suggested between his heart and the tree's heart. And, finally, ten of Joab's aides, armor bearers, circle around him as if he were animal prey and finish him off. Like Samson, he is somehow of nature even though his acts of deception and trickery—and in the case of Absalom his pretensions to hold monarchic power—mark him as very much a product of human culture. The hair suits him but is beautifully manipulated in this tale to suggest an antihero, not one meant to lead, not one who is divinely chosen, a fake—all hat and no cattle.

4

The Nazirite Vow

Domesticating Charisma and
Recontextualizing Hair

Many scholars would view the most important and informative passage dealing with Nazirite status to be Numbers 6, a text that describes a vow undertaken by an individual to become a Nazirite for a specified period of time. A close reading, with help from methodological perspectives introduced earlier, reveals a quite different version of Nazirism than that described for Samson with its underlying association between hair and manliness, warrior status, charisma, and divine selection. Some of these symbolic resonances of the Nazir's long hair may still reside in the culture associated with the phenomenon described in Numbers 6, motivating a person to assume a Nazirite vow, but the vow has been shaped by a particular priestly worldview that is highly concerned with issues of purity even while making holiness available to non-priests, or democratizing holy status. Although the book of Numbers contains more ancient materials, its current form and the contours of much of its content were probably determined by postexilic priestly writers of the Persian period, who shaped the work in a time without Judean kings and during subjugation by a foreign empire. They regarded the hereditary priesthood as the critical, stabilizing, and central remaining institution of leadership and guardian of the faith. They preserved ancient customs and ritual traditions while, in a more utopian fashion, reflect a vision of how the world should work. The worldview of such priests emerges in much of Numbers, and tracing the hair motif in context reinforces the suggestion of Martin Noth (1968) that "the Nazirite Law of Numbers is far removed from (the) old, original type of Naziriteship" exemplified by Samson and Samuel (54; see also Jastrow 1914). Long, uncut hair thus takes on particular connotations, while the vow involving hair reveals a different and later orientation than the one reflected in portrayals of biblical heroes discussed in chapter 3.

Turner Meets Numbers 6

Exegetical Level

What does the "native informant," the biblical narrator, reveal about Nazirite status? What information is emphasized? In Numbers 6, it is significant that the would-be Nazir may be a man or a woman. The vow to live as a Nazir is assumed voluntarily and is specially taken on. The verb describing the action of undertaking the vow is rooted in *pl'*, a term with miraculous or extraordinary nuances. The New Revised Standard Version (NRSV) translates "make a special vow" (cf. Leviticus 27:2 "make an explicit vow," NRSV). Brown et al. (1968 [hereafter cited as BDB]) suggest "do a difficult thing" or "make a hard vow." The person thus takes upon himself or herself an extraordinary, unusual responsibility through the means of a vow to God and under God. A Nazirite vow undertaken by an adult is, moreover, a temporary condition, and one sets the time limit.

The vow as described involves not cutting the hair and abstaining from wine and all grape products. The list of prohibited products is especially detailed including grapes, raisins, seeds, and skin (the last two terms are difficult to translate). The Nazirite status in Numbers 6 does not mention abstinence from unclean food. What is mentioned and emphasized is the avoidance of dead bodies, an important source of uncleanness.

Two rites of passage are described. One involves actions undertaken when the person under a Nazirite vow encounters a dead body; the other involves ritual passage at the time of the completion of the vow.

Operational Analysis

At the operational level, we ask what the Nazir does. He or she grows hair, presumably so that it shows. Is the implication that the ordinary person who has not undertaken such a vow trims his or her hair regularly? The question is especially pertinent for women, a matter to be discussed in its social, aesthetic, and literary contexts below. The operational question, difficult to answer, is how long is long? Would the avoidance of all grape products and the avoidance of funerary rituals, even those involving a father, mother, sister, or brother, be even more of a marker of a different or unusual status assumed by the person than the long hair?

At the level of what is done, we also explore more deeply the two ritual passages. In one, the vow is cut short because of contact with the dead. The hair connoting Nazirite status is cut off, as it is now contaminated (Numbers 6:9). Purification and burnt offerings make atonement for this unexpected interruption of the holiness. A guilt or reparation offering is provided, and the person begins his or her vow period over again.

At the normal completion of the promised time, he or she goes to the holy space, the tent of meeting, imagined here in a pretemple setting. A burnt offering of an unblemished young male lamb, a purification offering of an unblemished young ewe lamb, and a well-being offering of an unblemished ram, grain offerings of unleavened cakes made of fine flour and oil and matzos spread with oil, and drink offerings are presented. Then the head is shaved, and the hair of the Nazir's head is placed on the fire under the offering of well-being. A portion of the food offering is placed in the palm of the Nazir, to be transferred finally to the priest. It is as if the holiness reverts to the institutionalized holy person.

We have seen what the voluntary male or female Nazir does with the hair, growing it, then shaving it, and sacrificing it on the altar. Emphasis is placed on staying away from the impurity of death, and the list of grape-related products to be avoided is extended. The narrator describes two ritual patterns: The voluntary Nazir must interrupt his vow to acknowledge contact with death and restore purity through sacrifice, and he shaves his hair to begin the vow over again. At the completion of the uninterrupted vow, the Nazir undergoes a rite of passage involving sacrifice of pure and valuable animals in order to emerge from his or her extraordinary status. The hair itself, now shaved, is a critical part of the sacrifice, and drinking wine now asserts resumption of nonsacred, ordinary status.

Positional Analysis

The positional analysis is based on comparisons with images of Samson and Samuel, on an important oracle of the prophet Amos, and on the wider search for parallels and contrasts in language and content between Numbers 6 and other relevant passages. Also important is what can be reconstructed from biblical and extrabiblical evidence concerning the social context of Nazirism, as imagined in Numbers 6.

Formulaic language concerning the razor not going upon the head (Numbers 6:5) is found in tales of Samson (Judges 13:5; 16:17) and Samuel (1 Samuel 1:11). Perhaps most remarkable and surprising about Numbers 6, however, is that women as well as men can participate in being of "consecrated status" and that men and women can choose to bear this status. No divine charisma descends nor is a special quality implicit in being the child of a barren mother. This places Numbers 6 in strong contrast to tales of Samson and Samuel and to Amos's juxtaposition of the Nazir with the prophet, called by God. There is no hint of warrior status or political leadership. The term *pr'* is employed here as in Judges 5:2 and Deuteronomy 32:42, but rather than being linked to the male warrior's prowess, the long hair is linked to a temporary immersion into the sacred (Numbers 6:12, 13). To be sure, holy warriors upon whom the divine spirit descends are also immersed in holiness, but in the case of a Samson or a Samuel this descent is not a matter of an optional ritual status assumed by the would-be holy person. Its sudden, God-sent explosiveness is a kind of warrior's frenzy; in Number 6, matters are much more controlled. The Nazirite vow has the effect of domesticating, democratizing, or generalizing the possibility of Nazirite status. One need be able only to take the vow.

The vow is an interesting phenomenon in Israelite and later Rabbinic culture. A person makes an oath to the deity to do something, often promising to make a sacrifice involving some sort of self-denial or to provide a gift, giving of himself or herself in a way that goes beyond the usual requirements of liturgical law or custom. This vow allows one to prove devotion to the deity and perhaps is linked to expectations of reciprocity. Broken vows are serious matters that can lead to being cursed rather than being blessed.

One of the most famous and shocking biblical vows is undertaken by the judge Jephthah, who promises to the deity as a sacrifice whatever or whomever emerges to greet him after his victorious battle (Judges 11:29–40). Such battle vows are common in the war-rich tales of Israelite heroes. Unfortunately, the greeter is his daughter, but he dare not take back his vow. As the girl herself says, he has "opened his mouth" to God and must now do as promised. A similar story with a different outcome is that of Saul, who takes an oath upon himself and his troops not to eat food before they return in victory; those who disregard the oath must suffer the penalty of his curse. His own son, Jonathan, disregards the oath, and is saved from his father's wrath only by the people's intervention (1 Samuel 14:24–46).

The priestly writer of Numbers also describes an Israelite war vow at Numbers 21:1–3, and the notion of vowing there and elsewhere in scriptures underlies the whole tradition of the ban or *ḥerem* whereby Israelites vow to devote to destruction, that is to kill as an offering to the deity, all enemies defeated in battle in reciprocity for God's handing them their enemies. Inanimate spoil is often part of that which is banned as well, and those who covet and steal some of God's booty suffer the consequences of death, as in the tale of Achan in Joshua 7. Numbers 30 alludes to and provides a framework for more domesticated varieties of vowing, but these vows are to be taken just as seriously as those involving war, life, and death.

A man or a woman may take a vow to Yhwh upon themselves, although the latter may be subject to the approval of father or husband, depending upon her age and status. Only the widow or divorcee, who is no longer under the control of a man, may take upon herself vows as does an adult male. The lengthy passage concerning women's vows in Numbers 30 says almost nothing about the content of such vows and seems more concerned to clarify and circumscribe the woman's vow-taking capacity and her father or husband's veto power (30:3–15) than to describe the process of vowing or typical vows themselves. Nevertheless, it is clear that such pledges are binding (30:2), cannot be broken, and, as in the case of Jephthah's daughter, "according to all that comes forth from his mouth, he shall do" (30:2). It may be that husband or father is imagined to be able to veto a decision of a woman to become a Nazir or that the vow might be expected to be undertaken by a widow or divorcee rather than a woman tied to a man. Numbers 6 does not clarify.

The Nazirite vow, like other vows, however, is pictured to be undertaken with full seriousness, a kind of vow worn on the body, and one which must be properly completed. Awareness of the deep significance and often sacrificial nature of vows allows for an understanding of the way the hair is offered up and the way in which the interrupted vow must be resumed and properly completed. One might also suggest that the hair is invested with holiness. Like a whole burnt offering to the Lord, a special variety of sacrifice which is totally consumed by the flame, rising up to God in the smoke (see Leviticus 1:9), the hair needs to be transported to him in full by the fire. Holy hair cannot remain on earth once the period of sacred status has passed, nor can it remain attached to the now ordinary, wine-drinking person. The hair is divinely invested through the process of voicing the vow. The power of the word to transform is of special note. It is "opening the mouth" that makes the vow real and visceral. It is concrete in a world in which blessings and curses genuinely have the power to bring about what is spoken. By the same token, the hair is invested with the vow-taker's very person, his or her DNA, we might say, and thus is a way in which the Nazir offers himself or herself to the deity. The offered item is a substitute for the most valuable sacrifice of all, one's own person. The Nazirite vow in Numbers is thus deeply integrated into a particular priestly worldview involving the power of words, vowing, and literal offering of sacrifice. The notion of sacrifice may, indeed, always be implicit in the symbol of sacrally assumed long hair (see Hannah's vow in 1 Samuel 1:11 and the poetic juxtaposition of images of long hair and of freely offering oneself in Judges 5:2, where the term *pr'* is used as in Numbers 6:5). In Numbers 6, we see how priests place this custom within the contours of their own orientation to life.

The particular priestly orientation to hair customs in Numbers 6 also emerges in the emphasis on staying away from corpses during the vow. Priests in ancient Israel developed quite sophisticated notions of and rules pertaining to cleanness and uncleanness, purity and impurity, related ultimately to ritual roles in which the mediator between God and human had to be pure, approaching the purist of pure, which is the deity himself. One major source of contamination is death, the ultimate chaos, that which cannot be controlled. If death is a source of chaos, the most one can hope for is to contain that source, to demarcate one's immersion in it and one's cleansing and separation from it. While Numbers 19 portrays death as a source of chaos that exudes uncleanness from which all people need to be cleansed should they come in contact with it (see also Numbers 31:19), the priestly text of Leviticus 21:1–6 makes a special case for the avoidance of the dead on the part of the hereditary Aaronide priests, except for closest relatives. Notice that a hair custom of dishevelment or loosening (again the *pr'* root is used, here in the sense of flowing free rather than growing long; see chapter 3) is also associated with mourning in Leviticus 21. The priest is not to engage in wearing this sign of mourning, for an alteration of his hairstyle would signal the defilement of death and the very impermanence of life, that which is chaotic and mundane.

For the high priest, avoidance of the dead is even stricter, as seen in a comparison between Leviticus 21:1–3 pertaining to priests versus 21:10, pertaining to "the priest who is called above his fellows," (i.e., the high priest). He may not attend closely even to the bodies of his deceased mother or father. The same proscription applies to the Nazir. While under the vow, he or she may not defile himself or herself with death even should mother, father, sister, or brother die (Numbers 6:6–7), for "the set apart status of God is upon the head." That holiness must not be in touch with the uncleanness of death; pure wholeness must not touch chaos. Should the Nazir unavoidably come into contact with the dead, he or she must end the vow, shave the holy hair, emerge from sacred status, and recommence the vow period after the process of cleansing. The proscription against contact with the dead, which closely links priestly concerns with the version of the Nazirite status found in Numbers, is all the more serious and extreme in a culture in which kinship bonds are so central to identity and self-definition and in which death, as in so many cultures, is regarded as a core passage in the life of all human beings, one which family members attend and ease.

In a discussion of an Israelite "hierarchy of burial," Saul Olyan (2005) points to the positive and critical identity-defining connections between kinship and interment customs. For example, "an honorable burial in the family tomb was clearly the most to be desired" (2005, 602). The actual physical presence of those near and dear to the departed during ritual actions related to a kinsman's death is an important symbolic declaration of the visceral connection between the living and the dead and of the continuation of family and lineage. Such ceremonies include preparing the body for interment, the interment of the body, and participation in the final interment of the bones, a custom sometimes practiced in ancient Israel. Joshua Berman (2006) explores the important connections between burial customs and "identity politics" in the biblical telling of the death of Jacob. Thus lack of participation in ceremonies pertaining to the dead, even for a circumscribed period of time, is a significant way in which the Nazir is removed from a normal social role and one of several ways in which the Nazir of Numbers 6 is shaped by priestly preoccupations. No mention of avoidance of the dead is found in connection with Samson, and the proscription seems to belong to a later priestly layer in the development of the Nazirite vow. The Nazirite status paradoxically is both democratized to include any man or woman even while being made stricter in accordance with certain priestly concepts of clean and unclean.

The version of the wine prohibition which is part of the vow also reveals a particular late-biblical, priestly orientation. Notice that the priest, who must be in his most holy and "clean" condition in order to enter the sacred locus where God's spirit rests, the tent of meeting," is also not to "drink wine or strong drink" (Leviticus 10:8). The prohibition against drinking before engaging in his activities mediating between God and Israel has to do with the need for presence of mind and sobriety in undertaking sacrificial duties, but also, within the symbol system as described by the writer of Leviticus 10, is framed by the need to "distinguish between the holy and the common, and between the unclean and the clean." The Nazir, during his vow, is thus in a perpetual state of priestly-style cleanness and holiness, as if he were about to enter the sacred locus. The directive of the divine messenger to Samson's mother is that she not drink "wine or strong drink" (Judges 13:7) as the child develops within her. Judges 13:14 expands the prohibition to include anything that comes from the vine. In Numbers 6, however, a set of specific food products associated with the forbidden wine is listed, so that "wine" comes to include an extended list much as in the style of Rabbinic reasoning in which, for example, Passover proscriptions involving the avoidance of leavened bread during Passover come to include the avoidance of related foodstuffs. This extension of a prohibition by means of idea association is, in fact, typical of the priestly traditions of Numbers that underlie later developments in Jewish thought (see Jastrow 1914, 266; 269).

Equally interesting in a positional analysis is the lack of reference to unclean food in Numbers 6, a prohibition clearly found in Judges 13. Keeping kosher for the author of Numbers is a critical pan-Israelite means of self-definition, so basic that it need not be mentioned; it is assumed by the late priestly writer as customary for all Israelites.

The early material seems to allow Nazirite status to overlap with other sorts of sacred status. Samuel is a Nazir and a priest. Amos juxtaposes the Nazir with the prophet, and Samson, the Nazir, is also a swashbuckling superhero and warrior called a judge. Priestly roles are not mentioned in connection with the latter two instances of Nazirism. In Numbers 6, the divide between hereditary priesthood and voluntary Nazirism is clear, but the Levitical priests have control of many aspects of the process, especially due to the sacrifices that mark the interruption of the sacred status in case of contact with death and the conclusion of the specified period of time allotted for completion of the vow. It is the priest who officiates at the purification offering for the Nazir who has been contaminated (6:11), and the offering takes place at the special sacred locus over which priests preside, the tent of meeting. It is the priest who assures that the animals offered at the conclusion of the vow are pure, he who presents the offerings "before the Lord" (6:16), and he who finally receives the foodstuffs resulting from the sacrifice, as "a holy portion" (6:20). Both in terms of the emphasis on purity and in terms of the management of key ritual aspects of the vow, never mentioned, for example, in connection with Samson, the status of Nazirism, while available to any man or woman, is controlled by the hereditary priesthood in Numbers 6.

Scheper-Hughes and Lock's (1987) category of the "body politic" is relevant, for the priests, in a sense, take control of the Nazirite vow and the symbolism of the hair, which is finally sent heavenward in a thoroughly priestly ritual. One might say that the writers of Numbers would like to view Nazirite status as safely hijacked by the institutional, priestly establishment. The very availability of the vow to women makes it less of a threat. No charismatic, divinely selected leadership is assumed; rather, a person can take on a vow to display his or her piety and to experience temporarily that holiness that rightly belongs to priests as their hereditary purview, and the priests continue to serve as mediators between divine and human realms in the Nazirite process. This is in strong contrast to the direct relationship between God and Samson or God and

Samuel or the kind of direct tie between God and man imagined by Amos for those chosen to be Nazirites.

Charismatic Nazirites do not necessarily disappear after the classical period of Amos, and some may have considered themselves chosen from birth in settings of the sixth and fifth centuries BCE. No late biblical Nazir is described with certainty in the chronology of the preserved literature of the Hebrew Bible, although Jeremiah 7:29 and Zechariah 13:4, discussed in chapter 5, perhaps suggest some nuances of the holy associations of hairiness. For the most part, however, the charismatic Nazir seems to be located in earlier times, according to preserved traditions in the Hebrew Bible. It may well be that priestly leaders of the postexilic period sought to control the rise of charismatic holy men or to diminish their unique position by making the status of holiness available to everyone, a status surrounded by ritual actions that were controlled by the priests themselves. The priestly description of Nazirism in Numbers 6 may reflect, in fact, an implicit power struggle between various sources of political and religious power in Persian-period Judah. The hereditary priests, like Ezra, held power not only because of their particular Levitical genealogy, but also because of the support of Persia, conqueror of Israel. Others may have regarded themselves as holding power from God himself. The contrast is between the central, establishment, hereditary holy men and peripheral, perhaps antiestablishment charismatics. The Nazir could have been as much of a political threat to a Judean establishment as Samson was a military threat to the Philistines. One thinks here of the Christian holy men of late antique Byzantium who were a counterpoint of power to the bishops of the institutional church and the imperial bureaucracy (see Brown 1971, 95). Such figures are often thorns in the side of the establishment, and it is interesting that priestly elites here attempt to domesticate and contain the Nazirite role.

Who might be likely to take on this vow? What would the person get out of it? The questions posed by Obeyesekere (1981) concerning the emotional and personal content of the symbolism of hair are important, as is Scheper-Hughes and Lock's (1987) attention to the "individual body." Cultural and social context remain critical for a full understanding. The person who takes on the Nazirite vow needs to be able to provide some expensive offerings, a young male lamb if the vow goes awry because of contact with the dead, and several offerings at the conclusion of the vow. No allowance is made, as in other sacrifices, for less expensive substitutes (cf. Leviticus 12:8). One must assume, therefore, that the Nazir is imagined to be a person of some means for whom the loss of these animals would be possible. Such a person might be one of the landed gentry or ʿam hāʾāreṣ, "people of the land," perhaps one of the elders imagined to help in adjudicating local disputes at the gates of the city, the local power centers. In the postexilic and Persian periods, such a seeker of status might be one of the newly wealthy southerners, or Judeans, whose fortunes actually improved in the power vacuum created by the Babylonian conquest and the initial return after the exile. Only a relatively small number of elite Judeans were exiled, and an even smaller number returned. The various passages and situations of political and economic instability may well have led to the acquisition of new wealth in land on the part of those who stayed behind or who returned early after Cyrus's decree. These members of Judean society formed relationships with the hereditary priesthood (see Nehemiah 13:7, 28) and/or with the emissaries of the Persian central government, some of whom, like the leader, Ezra, were themselves priests. Alternatively, the custom of noncharismatic Nazirism may have developed in the Northern Kingdom of Israel, which scholars now believe was quite well off economically during the periods of Babylonian and Persian control and similar in cultural self-definition to the world of its southern brothers (see Knoppers 2006, 271–272; 279–280).

Leong Seow's (2007) analysis of the social world of the book of Ecclesiastes helps us speculate about the identity of those who might have desired to take on the Nazirite vow in the postexilic period. Using a variety of biblical and extrabiblical sources, Seow provides relevant detail about income, commercial enterprises, and other aspects of the economy of the Persian period. He points to "a new middle class" (4), a lively cash economy, the vitality of trade and other commercial activity, and "the democratization of commerce" (21) that led to newly rich members of society and also to the insecurities that come with volatile, vibrant economies. Today's newly rich could become tomorrow's impoverished debtor. Seow paints a socioeconomic portrait of haves and have-nots, the former often being favorites of the Persian-supported aristocracy who received grants from the king which they, in turn, could share with their allies. The newly rich, the insecurely rich, might well have the means and the desire to partake in the expression of religious devotion offered by the Nazirite vow. Nazirite status would allow such a person to exude and experience holiness, shoring up his or her sense of self-worth in the face of economic insecurity.

Women of means are also alluded to in biblical literature—for example in the description of the "woman of valor" in Proverbs 31. Drawing upon epigraphic, archaeological, and comparative material of the Persian period, Christine Yoder (2003) suggests that such a woman is pictured to engage in commerce, to have a successful cottage craft business, to run a complex household, to exercise considerable economic independence, and to hold high status in her family. Similarly, Avigad (1987) points to the existence of cylinder seals inscribed with women's names in pre- and postexilic periods (205–206). Since such seals were used to imprint stamps of ownership on material possessions or documents, they would indicate that the named women exercised independent economic and political power and that they had status in the public realm. Such women might also have the resources and desire to make a Nazirite vow and thereby assume the status related to it. Male or female, the person would be seeking to project an aura of holiness. Participation in the vow would probably add to his or her status, for the voluntary Nazir suggests, by his or her demeanor and behavior, not only that they have the means to take such a vow but also that they long for a sacred, closer-to-God experience.

To be sure, such vow takers may not merely be projecting sacredness to increase status in a community, but might well desire to be closer to the divine. Here we think of Obeyesekere's (1981) attention to the emotional dimension of religious symbolism. Not to drink wine with one's fellows, not to attend to the dead in one's community or one's family, and watching one's hair grow, would be reminders of and perhaps sources of a spiritual and psychological pilgrimage. Physical factors are involved as well. As Pnina Galpaz-Feller (2004) has suggested in explaining preferences among ancient Egyptian men to shave the head, the longer the hair, the more the lice, and the more the need for care and grooming. Long hair thus could well constantly remind the Nazir of his or her status and become a source of contemplation or preoccupation, much as in the case of Obeyesekere's long-haired female informants in Sri Lanka.

Interest in varieties of individual religious expression and preoccupation comes more and more to feature in ancient Israelite religion from the period just before the exile and afterward. In the works of the prophets Jeremiah, Ezekiel, and Deutero-Isaiah, one begins to see the emergence of a kind of confessional literature that includes autobiographic detail. The prophet Jeremiah, for example, personally addresses the deity about the experience of being a prophet.

> Found were your words, and I ate them,
> and became your word to me
> an exultation and the joy of my heart,
> for your name was proclaimed upon me,
> Yahweh, God of hosts.
> I did not sit among a klatch of players,
> and have a high time.
> Because of your hand, in isolation I sat,
> for with indignation you filled me.
> Why has my pain been enduring,
> and my wound sickly,

refusing to be healed?
Surely you are to me like a deceitful stream,
like waters that are unreliable.
(Jeremiah 15:16–18)

To be sure, the literary forms in which the prophets speak are conventionalized as in any traditional literature. The above passage, like many others that contain individual prayers, emotional content, and allusions to personal experience, is rooted in the form of the lament, but the personal stamp of the material is unmistakable (see also Jeremiah 20:7–18). The sixth-century BCE prophet Ezekiel and the seventh-century BCE prophet Jeremiah offer a critique of the notion that the children are punished for the sins of the parents (Ezekiel 18:2–4; Jeremiah 31:29–30). Sin is seen in more individual terms, whereby each person is punished for his own misdeeds. Job, a work that grapples with the issue of God's justice and one human being's undeserved suffering, is intensely engaged with the plight of the religious individual, seen apart from community guilt or a divine covenant with an entire people. Finally, the Persian-period memoir of Nehemiah, which includes large portions of the eponymous biblical book, is overtly autobiographic. In his memoir, Nehemiah, the governor of Judah, who is supported by the Persian government, describes his successes and failures in implementing his program. Within this context, a noncharismatic form of Nazirism might flower. The individual makes a choice to lead a particular kind of religiously conscious existence that sets him or her socially apart from the conviviality of drinking wine or the communal experience of mourning for friends and relatives, and he or she wears the sign of that status in his or her hairstyle.

Economic issues again are at play, for a noncharismatic Nazir in ancient Israel might be assumed also to have the leisure and wherewithal to contemplate and act upon this desire to be holy. Nazirism does not seem to be a community-supported status like the priesthood or the prophetic guild, which, as Robert Wilson (1980) has suggested, no doubt had its support groups, those who preserved what were regarded as valuable prophetic utterances (45; 76–83). One also thinks, for example, of the way in which the woman of Shunem supports the holy man Elisha. The vow to live as a Nazir for a certain length of time, taken upon himself or herself by the Nazir, is a self-selected condition by those in an economic and social position to do so. It is also entirely possible that the Nazirism of heroes such as Samson, with its associations of leadership, charisma, and victory in war, would be desirable traits for would-be community leaders. Even though I suggest that Numbers 6 is a later version of Nazirism than those presented by the authors of tales of Samson and Samuel and by the oracle of Amos, the traditions about the early long-haired heroes are part of the cultural tradition, available to the priestly authors of Numbers and actual members of the community whom they may picture to take on such a vow. Samson's Nazirism, however, is of a wild explosive variety, whereas the holiness in Numbers seems very controlled and circumscribed by priestly safeguards. How does the Nazirite vow described in Numbers 6 relate to images of hair, in particular, especially in comparison with images of Samson, for the hair would seem to be a critical part of what is projected?

Samson is a life-long Nazir so that, like a Sikh, his hair would be plentiful. He is portrayed as wearing it in plaits as discussed in chapter 3. There may have been various accepted hairstyles for the manly charismatic Nazir. Unless the Nazir of Numbers 6 took on the vow for a number of years, the length of the hair really would not have been noticeable, unless Israelite men wore their hair cropped enough that even several months' growth would be apparent. Pictorial evidence of premonarchic periods and for the ninth century BCE suggests that men's hair was at least shoulder length. The Lachish reliefs of the eighth century BCE portray the hair of some of the men who fight for Judah as covered by hats, wraps, or helmets; the length of their hair is not clearly ascertainable. Others, who wear no head covering, have cropped hair in tight curls, but as discussed, there are questions about the Judean versus Nubian or Egyptian identity of the men with visible, short hair. If such portrayals are accurate representations of Judeans, then the uncut hair of the voluntary Nazir would more quickly become an apparent sign of a change in status. The shaving of the head, marking that the person had been under a Nazirite vow (or in mourning), would have been the more dramatic and sudden indication of transition. Abstaining from the social activity of drinking wine and not attending to funerary rites of friends or relatives may well have been the more effective and obvious daily statements of a man's temporary set-aside status, with its priestly and sacred connotations, than the slow growing of hair. The same might be said for women.

We have no evidence that women wore their hair short. To the contrary, the Song of Songs describes the beautiful long hair of a young woman, while the woman accused of adultery has her hair let down, so presumably it is long enough to put up. Pictorial evidence from the eighth century BCE portrays Judean women of Lachish wearing long cloth headdresses that completely cover the hair. Thus it is possible that in public neither the growing nor the shaving of hair would have been visible. The woman's abstaining from wine and her lack of attendance to funerary rites might be better indicators. There is some evidence, in fact, that women were especially involved in rites of mourning (Jeremiah 9:16–17; see King and Stager 2001, 373). Thus the hair may have been secondary to other symbolic manifestations of Nazirism in the view of the priestly writers of Numbers 6.

In dealing with positional analysis or context, which has led to priestly interests and motifs in Numbers 6, and in considering in context the perspective of the person who takes the vow, a special comment on women is necessary. Numbers 6 opens Nazirism to both genders, radically altering the symbolic web linking Nazirism, hairiness, and maleness and discussed in chapter 3. Such a view both democratizes and domesticates holy status, even while perhaps reducing its charisma and potency. It is important also to mention that the Levitical priesthood, both in Numbers and Leviticus, does not include women in the ranks of priests. A woman of priestly family can partake of food resulting from special priestly offering and, to that extent, she can partake of the holiness, but she is not a priest. In fact, an interesting passage in Numbers 12 viscerally puts Miriam of the priestly tribe of Levi, sister of Moses and Aaron, in her place. While in some genealogical references, she is listed as having special leadership status (Micah 6:4; 1 Chronicles 5:29 [6:3 in English]), and is called a prophet in Exodus 15:20–21, Numbers 12 emphasizes the punishment of Miriam for speaking out against the exclusive priestly leadership of her brother Moses. This passage has been understood to suggest that there may have been priestly clans at some point in the history of Israel, claiming descent from Miriam the Levite or a history of women priests now edited out of the surviving literature of the Bible. Could it be that the priestly authors of Numbers allow women the safe, compensatory holiness of Nazirite status? Paradoxically, this form of Nazirism allows priestly leaders to give women of means an opportunity for some kind of sacred status, but it is temporary and is not a threat to the male, Levitical priesthood. Voluntary Nazirism makes it clear, further, that male Nazirites are no competition for the male hereditary priests because even women may assume the holiness. Priestly writers of similar orientation may well be responsible for the first creation account of the Bible, in which both male and female are created in the image of God, and no hierarchy is emphasized between men and women. Such a text is oddly inclusive of women and potentially exclusive at the same time, for the status has to do with primordial times and is no threat to actual social reality. The image makes women feel a part of divine creation without promising them power.

5

Absent Hair

Chapter 3 explored the juxtaposition of maleness, virility, warrior status, and special chosen status that emerges in attitudes toward hair in the Nazirism of Samson and Samuel, in the pretensions of the would-be king/hero Absalom, and in the poetic implications of Judges 5:2 and Deuteronomy 32:42. Chapter 4 dealt with developments and changes in the concept of Nazirism that reflect the worldview of the postexilic priestly writers of Numbers and traced the ways in which the hair itself comes to play a different role in Nazirite status. The hair continues to be a cultural code, but the culture of these writers and their use of hair as symbol changes. In each case, the hair leads to a range of additional symbols and motifs and relates to views of Israelite identity, concepts of holiness, and attitudes toward gender. Hair is integral to the ways in which biblical writers project and construct ideas of self-definition. While the growing of hair has critical meanings, the shaving or cutting of hair, whether self-imposed or externally imposed, is equally meaningful, as seen in tales of Samson and in the ritual processes related to the Nazirite vow.

Another set of biblical texts has to do with the loss or absence of hair: the tale of David's envoys in 2 Samuel 10:4–5; related texts concerning conquest and images of shaving; texts discussing mourning practices and other ritual passages; and the significant contrasts drawn by biblical writers between "hairy" men and "smooth" men: Esau and Jacob, Elijah and Elisha, and Joseph as prisoner versus Joseph as servant of Pharaoh. Saul Olyan (1998) has explored a number these texts with insight, cautioning the reader to pay special attention to shaving in context. He notes that many passages concerning the elimination of hair have to do with some sort of alteration in status, whether it is a return to a state of purity after a period of uncleanness, a marking of the death of a loved one and the reintegration to the realm of the living after that person's demise, or a forced integration into the people Israel on the part of a conquered maiden who must leave her old world behind. I return to these issues of alteration and aggregation later, but first closely examine 2 Samuel 10:4–5 and its variant in 1 Chronicles 19:4.

Unmanning Hair

Like Judges 16, which relates the tale of Samson and Delilah, 2 Samuel 10 presents a story involving the imposed cutting of hair against the person's will, in this case the shaving of men's beards. The passage raises important issues concerning shame and honor in androcentric societies and the perceived capacity to control one's own destiny and to lead others. The reactions of the men to the imposed loss of their facial hair, of King David to the treatment of his emissaries, and of the people Israel to the implications of this exchange speak to critical issues in worldview and self-definition, all contained in the symbolism of hair.

Events begin when David sends officials, members of the court, to offer his condolences at the death of a neighboring monarch, the King of Ammon. Advisors to the dead king's son, his successor, convince him that the emissaries have come to spy and to lay the groundwork for an insurgency in this time of transition. They decide to put the visitors in their place: The Masoretic version of 2 Samuel 10:4–5 has the Ammonites shave off half the beards of the Israelite envoys and cut their robes in half, at their rear ends, whereas the variant in 1 Chronicles 19:4 has the Ammonites "shave them" and cut the robes in half up to the hip or buttocks (see also Septuagint (LXX): "shaved off their beards."). The version in the Masoretic Text (MT) may have originated as a repetition of the word "half" that goes with the robe- cutting in all versions, but the resulting reading in MT makes even more of a spectacle of the diplomats, having them become clownlike in appearance. The goal in either case is humiliation and suggests a particular attitude to men's facial hair in ancient Israel. The beard is a sign of male identity. To have the beard or half the beard removed against one's wishes by foreign enemies, together with the symbolic ripping of the clothes up to an erogenous zone, betokens exposure, vulnerability, and being turned into a womanlike figure who is sexually used by male enemies. Sexual and gender nuances are clear; the relationship between Ammonites and Israelites is not one of equality but one of domination and submission. To feminize the man is indeed the goal.

An important motif in an international array of epic literatures, explored by Emily Vermeule (1979) for ancient Greek literature and by David Shulman (1986) for Tamil traditions, portrays the loser in battle as the one who is made into a raped woman. This is a common motif in Hebrew Bible as well, as I have shown in a study of Jael's defeat of the enemy general Sisera (Niditch 1989). Here, ironically, the warrior is a woman who subdues the male general in images laden with eroticism and death. She overpowers, feminizes, and defeats him. A similar phenomenon is found in the relationship between Samson and Delilah and the role of haircutting in this very traditional theme (see Niditch 1990).

The juxtaposition of robe ripping and beard cutting is important in imagery of the feminization of the enemy. The ripped garment appears with similar connotations in a scene in 1 Samuel 24:1–7. At this point in the rivalry between Saul and David, the would-be usurper of his throne, David learns that Saul is relieving himself in a nearby cave. The phrase that refers to this activity of eliminating bodily waste might literally be translated either "covering his feet," to reflect the position assumed for defecation, or "pouring out his 'legs/feet.'" The legs or feet are sometimes a euphemism for genitals and so the phrase may refer to urination. In either event, the king is vulnerable and exposed, and it is in this context that David softly sneaks up (the "softly" term is used in an intimate and erotic setting, as Ruth softly comes to Boaz at the threshing floor [Ruth 3:7]; see also the murder of Sisera by the guerilla woman warrior Jael in Judges 4:21) and tears off the bottom of Saul's robe. He will no longer be able properly to cover himself. That David's action is an assertion of power with connotations of unmanning is clear from the younger man's guilt following the event. He has not killed the king as urged by his fellows, but he has thoroughly humiliated him as he himself implies (1 Samuel 24:7).

A second version of this type of scene in 1 Samuel 26:7–12 seems to reflect some of this guilt; it softens the sexual connotation. Saul is vulnerable, but only because he sleeps deeply in the cave, in the tardēmāh of Yhwh, a special trance state that is the work of the deity (cf. Adam in Genesis 2:21 and Abraham in Genesis 15:12). No mention is made of embarrassing positions or activities that heighten erotic nuances. Nor is the robe cut. The younger man takes only the spear and water jar, both personal possessions marking identity, but ones that are less associated with the bodily functions. Instead, the spear and jar function as recognition tokens in a traditional pattern (as in the case of the signet, chord, and staff in the tale of Tamar and Judah in Genesis 38). David is able with these possessions to indicate that he was with Saul and spared him

(1 Samuel 26:16–17). David shows Saul a recognition token, the corner of his garment, in the conclusion of the version in chapter 24 as well, but the piece of cloth in the initial scene indicates more than identity; it connotes a stripping and a symbolic act of emasculation.

The scene in 2 Samuel 10 includes not only the motif of ripping the bottom of the robe but also the shaving of facial hair. Scholars have wisely cautioned that shaving hair against a person's will need not always connote a castration of sorts, for the heads of women captives are shaved (Hallpike 1969) in Deuteronomy 21. As Olyan (1998) suggests, all these instances have to do with some sort of alteration in status and, in the cases of the women captives, Samson, and David's emissaries, with undesired, forced alterations, with the loss of a desired status. Given that beards are only grown by men, however, their loss in a culture which valorizes men's facial hair is a special affront with gendered connotations. Cynthia Chapman (2004) points to a similar conceptual complex at play in Assyrian culture (26, 39, 47). The bald cheek is a sign of having been bested in a contest and made a woman. The narrator of 2 Samuel implies as much. He observes about the envoys, "for the men were intensely ashamed, and the king said, 'Return to Jericho until your beards grow back,' and they returned." They do not want to be seen. The action of the Ammonites incenses King David, for the emissaries are an extension of his person and his power, and he goes to war and roundly defeats the Ammonites. The shaved beard and the ripped robe are potent symbols; the Israelites will not allow themselves to be unmanned or overpowered; that they are mere women is, on the other hand, precisely the message that the ill-fated Ammonites sought to send. The Ammonites clearly miscalculate; instead of putting the Israelites in their place, they commence a spiral of violence whereby visceral symbolic actions escalate to all-out war.

The individual body, the social body, and the body politic are at play in the scene concerning David's shaved envoys, as in tales of Samson. The men respond emotionally and viscerally to the forced removal of their hair, a response the king fully understands and with which he identifies. The responses only make sense within a cultural context that equates male power with facial hair, the loss of hair with loss of power. As in the imposed wearing of the queue, the forced removal of hair symbolizes political control. The Ammonites force the Israelite emissaries, substitutes for the king himself, to wear the bare cheek imposed upon them. They become a walking symbol of defeat and humiliation and of the enemies' power.

This interpretation of the shaved cheek is reinforced by a brief image of conquest employed by the eighth-century BCE prophet Isaiah. Language that refers to shaving and the razor and reference to the body parts which are shaved create a physical, bodily metaphor for consummate defeat and play very overtly on erotic elements of manhood. The oracle predicts an invasion by king of the superpower, Assyria: "On that day the Lord will shave with a razor, hired in 'across the River,' via the king of Assyria, the head and the pubic hair [literally the hair of the 'legs or feet']. And the beard, it will sweep away" (Isaiah 7:20).

Traditional literature is such that a piece often stands for the whole. John Foley (1991) has shown how a particular color or a single motif or a thread of language, when loaded with cultural meanings, shared and recognized by authors and their audiences, bring to bear on the context the broader tradition with all its "immanent referentiality." This brief oracular pronouncement thus draws upon the meanings of hair cutting, in particular the forced cutting of the hair of the cheek and pubic areas, to create an image of subjugation and loss of power associated with the virility of the warrior. Second Samuel 10 describes the victims' response to what has been done to them and reveals the way in which David allows them time to recover; the reader receives an impression of the men's gut response to the loss of their beards. An emotional response attaches here as well to the mere mention of hair-cutting in a battle context. The coupling of pubic hair with head hair and beard in Isaiah 10 gives further evidence of the visceral nuances associated with the forced cutting of adult men's body hair. Each of these texts provides a window into the larger tradition and partakes of it in its own way. Context is critical, however. How does self-imposed or the accepted removal of hair at times of mourning or in a variety of ritual contexts relate to the symbolic complexes explored thus far?

Mourning Hair

Numbers 6 presents one case of hair-cutting within the context of a voluntary vow. The Nazir must terminate the vow by shaving the hair should he or she come into contact with a corpse, and the normal period of the vow is terminated by ritual actions that involve shaving. As noted in chapter 4, the person's temporary sacred status is invested in the hair. Traditional nuances of Nazirite hair that pertain to divinely selected warrior heroes such as Samson might influence what is projected by the Nazir and how others respond to him or her. Individual, operational, and positional analyses and interest in both the personal and the public dimensions of the long hair and the cutting of the hair inform our work. I have also discussed the hair as a sacrifice and the way in which, as Olyan (1998) has suggested, shaving leads to a change in status, in this case a return to mundane status and reintegration into the workaday world of ordinary hair. Whether shaving because of contact with a corpse or at the end of the vow, the person who voluntarily assumes Nazirite status is starting over as a Nazir or as a non-Nazir. The cutting of hair in connection with death has thus already been introduced in the discussion of Numbers 6 and is another important aspect of our discussion of "absent hair."

The cultures of the ancient Near East, like many contemporary cultures, marked the passage of loved ones from the realm of the living to the dead in various ritual ways. Biblical descriptions of the state of mourning, both among Israelites and their neighbors, heavily invoke embodied codes, messages worn on the bodies of mourners. Hair, whether shaved, cut, or disheveled, plays an important role. The various descriptions of mourning practices in their fullest and most bodily versions involve three components: the balding of the head; the cutting or clipping of the beard; and the gashing of the flesh. Not all biblical descriptions include all three components, and various equivalent Hebrew terms are used for balding, shearing, and shaving. Sometimes the tearing of clothes and/or wearing of sackcloth accompany the cutting of flesh, whereas in other cases these clothing practices may be a milder symbolic substitute for the tearing of the body itself. Similarly, dishevelment of hair or partial shaving may replace complete shaving.

Customs described for non-Israelites parallel those of Israelites, and a few motifs may stand for the larger cluster, declaring that someone close to the bearer of the symbols has died. The reference to the loss of hair is, in fact, the most consistent and essential of the symbolic complex. Job 1:20 describes the suffering protagonist's ritual actions when he learns that his sons and daughters have been killed in a kind of tornado.

> And he tore his robe,
> and he shaved his head.

The eighth-century BCE prophet Isaiah describes national mourning by Israel's southeastern neighbor, Moab,

> On every head baldness,
> every beard is clipped.
> (Isaiah 15:2)

The exilic period prophet Jeremiah describes mourning in Gaza: "Baldness has come to Gaza.... How long will you gash yourselves" (Jeremiah 47:5). In one of the fullest descriptions of mourning, Jeremiah writes of Moab,

> For every head is bald
> and every beard is clipped,
> on all hands are gashes,

and on the loins sackcloth.
(Jeremiah 48:37)

Notice the specific formula shared by the eighth- and sixth-century BCE prophets.

A similar constellation of motifs applies to Israelite mourners in a lengthy trajectory of texts. In Jeremiah 41:5, Northern pilgrims come to Jerusalem during the turbulent events surrounding the Babylonian invasions wearing the conventionalized demeanor of mourners, "shaved of beard, clothes torn, and gashed." Similarly, Ezekiel describes the state of mourning predicted after Israel suffers divine punishment for having broken its covenant with God:

> And they will gird in sackcloth,
> and cover them will shuddering,
> and on every face is shame,
> and upon all their heads, baldness.
> (Ezekiel 7:18)

Shuddering and shame are the emotions that accompany sackcloth and balding. Punishments bring death by pestilence, war, and famine (Ezekiel 7:15), and death requires ritual balding. The balding motif that marks death in reference to Israelites is found also in Micah 1:16, a prophetic text of the classical period of the eighth century BCE, and in Jeremiah 7:29 and 16:6 and Ezekiel 5. The latter three passages from exilic-period prophets are particularly interesting in referential meanings and conceptual reach. Jeremiah 7:29 employs the term *nezer* for the hair which is shed, raising issues about the meanings of consecration that attach in this particular context. Ezekiel 5 offers a dramatic scene in which God commands the prophet to remove hair by passing a sharp blade or sword over his head and beard and then engage in a variety of ritual actions with the cut hair. Jeremiah 16:6, read in context, provides another important entry into the emotional and cultural meanings of shaved hair in mourning.

Jeremiah 7:29

The words of God in Jeremiah 7:29 are set out in stylized, parallel speech, typical of the heightened language of the deity. In the Hebrew of Jeremiah 7:29, the verb and the suffix attached to *nezer* are in the feminine singular. Micah 1:16, which includes the verbs "shear" and "make bald" but no noun for the hair, also employs the feminine singular form of the verb.

> Shear off your *nezer* [Nazirite hair/lock]
> and throw it away,

and raise on the barren heights a lament.

(Jeremiah 7:29)

To whom does the deity speak? Israel is personified as a woman in Micah 1:13, the section that includes the order to make bald and to shear hair. She is the "daughter of Zion." The city, land, or people as a whole are personified as feminine, and Jeremiah and other prophets call Israel an unfaithful wife (see Holladay 1986, 266). In the Masoretic Hebrew version of Jeremiah 7:29, perhaps influenced by the classical text in Micah 1:16 (which is one version of a formulaic phrase related to mourning), women are imagined to shear their hair in mourning like men. As seen in Ezekiel 7, covenant faithlessness brings destruction and death, and the shaved head is a symbol of the resulting state of mourning. Jeremiah, who, like Ezekiel, writes during the time of Babylonian conquest, sees Israel's suffering as the deserved wages of sinful behavior. The specific reference to the *nezer* would seem to suggest the variety of Nazirism outlined in the priestly text of Numbers 6; the Nazirite vow is available to men and women and is interrupted by contact with death during the vow period, an interpretation explored by William Holladay (1986, 266). The temporary consecration is to be cut short.

An alternative range of meanings for the reference to cut hair in Jeremiah 7:29 emerges in the ancient Greek translations of Hebrew versions of Jeremiah. Since the Greek does not differentiate between the masculine and feminine in the imperative or in the possessive pronoun "your," the text reads as if the object of the oracle were masculine. Readers of the Greek traditions thus might have assumed that the oracle is directed to the prophet himself. Some of the Greek manuscript traditions do not use the term *nezer* but use more neutral terms for hair. One important manuscript tradition, Sinaiticus, however, describes the hair much more specifically as "the hair of the holiness of your Nazirite status." The implication might be that Jeremiah is a Nazir, like Samson and Samuel, and that he wears his hair long in the style of the Nazir. Jeremiah 1:5, the first oracle of the book that serves as the prophet's initiation, has God speak to the prophet thus,

Before I formed you in the womb,
I knew you,
and before you emerged from the uterus,
I sanctified you.
A prophet to the nations
I appointed you.

The special selection and consecration of Jeremiah, even before his birth, might well suggest that this reference to casting away the *nezer* is more than metaphoric. He is presented as a consecrated, holy man who is told that he can no longer bear the sign of his holiness in this time of death, destruction, and broken covenant. God's instructions to shear his *nezer* and throw it away may in fact be directions for a sign act involving hair.

The prophetic sign act is a symbolic and dramatic enactment that physically and often viscerally has the prophet represent a particular message from God. When commenting on the future rather than a present condition, the very representation helps bring about that which it predicts in a sympathetic magical way. We will look at another lengthier and more complicated sixth-century BCE sign act involving a prophet's hair in a moment, but even this brief command to shear and throw away hair is evocative and powerful. No ordinary term is used for the hair. The hair has special connotations; its removal betokens more than mourning. The tossing away of this holy hair betokens a loss of consecration, a distance from God. The prophet's loss of his sign of consecration, perhaps preordained and worn from birth, predicts and helps bring about a loss of divine presence.

If the oracle is addressed to Israel, the *nezer* takes on related metaphoric meaning. Jeremiah is preparing the people for mourning; their sins have caught up with them, and soon they must acknowledge the deaths around them with shorn hair. That the hair is called *nezer,* however, again suggests a loss of consecration and holiness, a distancing from their sacred covenant partner, the Lord. Special hair implies special status, the loss of hair the loss of that status, a rupture of identity as God's people, and mourning over the defeat of Israel, the chosen people, and the fall of Jerusalem, the holy place.

Ezekiel 5

While the term of consecration is not used for hair in Ezekiel 5, the context for hair cutting is the same: defeat in war and conquest by the Babylonians. Ezekiel 5 presents a powerful sign act involving hair; its ritual dimensions are explicit and arresting. The prophet imagines God to order him to take a blade like a barber's razor and run it over his head and beard. The term used for the blade literally means sword and thus evokes the context of war. The image of Ezekiel shaving with a sword and the ritual actions which are to follow almost suggest the sort of mythical scenes found in Zhang Yimou's 2002 film *Hero.* Ezekiel is to take the severed hair and divide it into three parts. A third is to be burned once the siege is complete; a third is to be taken and "struck with the sword" around the city; a third is to be scattered to the wind. Other bits of the hair are to be set aside and fixed in the skirt of the prophet's robe; then another small portion of the hair which had been set aside is to be thrown upon the fire. The hair acts as a combustible that creates a conflagration that attacks "all the house of Israel."

The meaning of the opening sign act is laid out clearly: a third of the people will die of pestilence or famine, a third will fall by the sword, and a third will be exiled. Thus the prophet's hair symbolizes the people; his own personal identity is fused with that of his people, and, as seen throughout our study, hair often serves to mark identity. A part of the body, hair metonymically represents the whole. Here the prophet represents the people as well. They will suffer death, destruction in war, and exile. Through the symbolic action, the prediction and the manipulation of the symbolic hair help bring about the destruction. God imposes hair cutting on the prophet, who must do the deity's bidding. It is clear, as in 2 Samuel 10, where the power lies. The loss of hair again is suggestive of loss of life and mourning, as in so many biblical passages, but here it does not invoke pity or hopes of beginning over. It is a source of destruction.

The cut hair operates on many levels: it is a universal source of identity; it is culturally related to mourning practices; the power to cut it suggests the assertion of other sorts of power. Infused with the essence of personal identity—in this case a corporate identity in which the prophet identifies with his people—it can be magically manipulated in a ritual context to bring about a particular dark future. The hair hidden in the robe and thrown on the fire is not interpreted within the scene but perhaps refers to a remnant spared, on the one hand, and to the people's responsibility for the chaos of conquest on the other. Their sin has been the source of the fire that consumes them; they are destroyed because of the nature of their beings, corrupted and unfaithful to the covenant with God. As seen in Jeremiah 7, they are no longer holy, God's people, but are detached, unclean, and dangerous, like the hair itself. Ezekiel symbolically throws them on the fire, and like a flammable material, they spread destruction.

Jeremiah 16:6

Another series of oracular pronouncements in the book of Jeremiah, a prophet who seems most interested in the symbolism of hair, provides a particularly rich description of mourning practices (Jeremiah 16:2–9). In the chaotic, upside-down world of defeat and conquest, no mourning practices will be possible:

> And die will great ones and small ones in this land.
> They will not be buried, and no one will lament them;

> no one will be gashed;
> no one will be made bald for them. (16:6)

The oracle goes on to describe other aspects of the mourning ritual that shall not be engaged in: breaking (bread) for the mourner, offering comfort, giving "the cup of consolation" for their mothers and fathers, and feasting. And then, finally, after this lengthy description of ancient Israelite funerary practice, the prophet adds that the "voice of exultation and the voice of joy, the voice of the bridegroom and the voice of the bride" will be eliminated. In language reminiscent of the apocalyptic conclusion to the book of Ecclesiastes, weddings, too, are to be banished. Thus key ritual passages marking the beginning of new life and joy and the end of life with attendant sadness and acts of consolation are to be interrupted in a world of chaos.

The act of shaving one's hair takes its place among key cultural symbols that allow for life to go on. One must mark the end of one period in which the deceased lived, acknowledge his or her parting, comfort his or her loved ones, and move on. As the hair grows back, as the wounds of the gashing heal, renewal takes place. This is to participate in the normal cycle of life. Loss is to be suffered; the loved one, like the mourners' hair, is severed from the living and, like the symbolic lacerations, leaves a wound in his loved ones, but regrowth and healing follow. Jeremiah's oracle is visceral and shocking because it predicts that this normal cultural pattern will be utterly interrupted. The symbolic actions that Israelites have used to make critical transitions in life will not be available to them in the chaos of Babylonian conquest. Death, unmarked and unmourned, is an ultimate punishment. One sees how important the symbolism of absent hair is in the context of mourning. On a personal or individual level, the shaved person is recognized as one who needs comfort, who has suffered loss, and one who has dutifully attended to the dead. The mourner projects his or her rightful place within the rhythms of the culture and is a reminder of the one who has died. The shaven head thus serves to reinforce critical ideas of community and culture. To eliminate this symbol is to lose a thread in one's personal and cultural identity. The symbol of absent hair in the wake of death is, moreover, a long-standing one.

Even as late as the fifth-century BCE prophet Ezra, the balding of hair and beard indicates literal or symbolic mourning. When the conservative priest-leader of the returned community learns that the people have not "separated from the people of the land," engaging in what he regards as forbidden intermarriage, he shows his displeasure in acts of mourning. It is as if the culture is at risk of death, and, indeed, in his view, the community tempts God to impose new punishments. Thus Ezra tears his clothing and removes the hair of his head and his beard (Ezra 9:3). Although shaving off the hair in the context of death seems to be common in the ancient Near East and Israel throughout the biblical period, some groups reject this custom involving hair, either for all Israelites or for certain members of the community who differentiate themselves and their own special status within the people by not participating in the custom of hair removal to mark death.

Limitations on Signs of Mourning Involving Hair

Leviticus 21:5, 10, and 11 discuss mourning and hair cutting in relation to hereditary Levitical priests. Interesting aspects of this passage include (1) the distinctions drawn between ordinary men and priests in relation to body customs that mark the condition of mourning; (2) the further distinctions, reflected in hair and other body customs, between ordinary priests and the high priest; and (3) implicit assumptions about the ways in which ordinary people wear the state of mourning.

Leviticus 21:5 has been interpreted in various Jewish circles as a command to grow *peyes,* long side-locks still worn today among certain Hasidic groups. It is clear from the biblical context, however, that the verse applies only to priests and in the context of mourning. The priest is to avoid contact with the dead and the uncleanness that results from that contact, except when the deceased is among the nearest of blood relatives—the mother, father, son, daughter, or virgin sister (21:1–3). In all cases, however, the priest is to eschew bodily customs of mourning, balding, and gashing. It is thus assumed that nonpriests would bear these signs after the death of a loved one. The beard, too, is apparently diminished among nonpriestly men in the context of mourning: the edges are shaved, contrary to the usual fuller way of wearing the beard. This partial cutting is perhaps a less intrusive version of eliminating hair than complete shaving (cf. Isaiah 15:2; Jeremiah 41:5) and seems to indicate a variation in the mourning custom of hair removal. Even the partial cutting of the beard, however, would mark the male mourner, indicating loss, the change of status and identity, and the need to regrow and regenerate. He sends a message that he has been reduced and changed by the loss of a loved one but will slowly rejoin the mainstream of society (like the men of 2 Samuel 10 who involuntarily lose their beards or part of them to enemies).

The reason for the priest's avoidance of hair cutting is found in Leviticus 21:6. The priest is "holy," set apart, a mediator between God and Israel, and must maintain a constant state of ritual purity. As Mary Douglas (1966) has shown, holiness is related symbolically to bodily wholeness (52–54). Thus the priest needs to maintain bodily boundaries demarcated by intact hair and body. He must not, moreover, look like a mourner who is by definition unclean because of contact with the dead, death being a major source of uncleanness in priestly threads of Israelite religion. His cultural and socio-structural role thus forbids him to partake of certain mourning customs and overrides the personal and emotional need and the cultural expectation that one will display signs of loss and removal from one's usual status after the death of a loved one.

The high priest is even more holy than the priest, and thus his relation to death and to the manipulation of hair in connection with death is even more circumscribed. He is not to "defile himself" (i.e., come into contact with the dead), even for either of his parents. As to bodily customs, he is directed not to dishevel his hair or to tear his garments (Leviticus 21:11). These treatments would seem to be one step removed from actual balding of the head and gashing of the flesh itself. Perhaps ordinary priests would be allowed such non-invasive substitutes, but not the high priest. Even these signs interrupt his wholeness and holy status.

Hair customs related to mourning thus mark a hierarchy of status between people and priest and between priest and high priest. Two other passages seem to extend the prohibition of mourning customs involving hair to all Israelites, for to such writers all Israelites are holy. Israel, moreover, is to distinguish itself from its neighbors via hair, a thread in ethnic self-definition discussed in chapters 2 and 3.

Deuteronomy is a biblical book of Levitical origins that purports to be Moses's final testament to the people Israel. Moses reviews the history of the people, gathers together a set of legal and liturgical materials, and provides a theological overview of the covenantal bond between God and his people. The authors of Deuteronomy imagine a theocracy in which God's people will be governed by divine law; all are the children of God, "holy to the Lord," set apart and distinguished from foreigners. It is within such a context in which Israel is described as God's "treasured possession," "chosen out of all the peoples on earth," that we find the command,

> Do not gash yourselves.
> Do not place baldness between your eyes for the dead.

The authors of Deuteronomy 14:1 seem to suggest that, in the cultural world with which they are familiar, mourning could be marked both by cutting the flesh and by cutting a frontal portion of one's hair. As in Leviticus 21:5, only a portion of the hair (in the case of Leviticus 21:5, a portion of facial hair) is cut. For the writers of Deuteronomy 14:1, all Israelites are holy and priestlike. As in the case of the Nazirite vow outlined in Numbers 6, holiness is democratized.

Similar in conception is Leviticus 19:27–28, which describes mourning customs that purposefully disrupt the wholeness of the body. Again, partial balding and beard shaving seem to be the customs that are rejected for all Israelites, along with more invasive bodily change:

> Do not go around the edges of your head,
> and do not destroy the edges of your beard,
> and marks of scarification to the person, do not make in your flesh,
> and the writing of incision [i.e., tattoos], do not make upon
>   yourselves.

Although death is not mentioned in Leviticus 19:27–28, and verse 28 has been taken by Jews as a general prohibition on tattoos, the gashing and two varieties of hair cutting are a formulaic cluster that suggest mourning customs. The cutting of hair and beard cutting again appear to be a partial or token cutting rather than a full shaving. The hair of the head seems to be cut around each of the temples or in a row from temple to temple. The tattoo seems to be an additional way of incorporating the deceased into one's very body, so that he or she never completely disappears. What is incised may have been a name, letter, or symbol. Like the gash, the tattoo will heal, but both leave marks or scars. The tattoo is thus a way to mark the death of a loved one, more permanent than hair cutting and more visible than the scar from gashing. The mourner will return to his or her daily life, renewed but changed; his or her emotional transformation and the loss of a person to the social group are marked with a permanent interruption of the contours of the body. The writers of Leviticus 19, however, reject all four signs of mourning, permanent or transitory. Again, the issue is holiness as wholeness (19:2), but it is now applied not only to priests, but to all Israelites.

It is also of interest in this context that various foreigners are directly identified by hairstyles involving a special trimming or clipping of the hair at the temples. Certain desert folk are described three times in Jeremiah as those who are "clipped off at the temples" (see Jeremiah 9:25; 25:23, and 49:32). In contrast to the Moabites and others mentioned by Jeremiah, these people are given no name. They are the people of a certain hairstyle. We have explored throughout the book the ways in which hair betokens the ethnic identity of those inside the group and those outside of it, and it is interesting to find passages that describe a group by their ecosystem and their hair. The writers of Leviticus 19:27–28 urge Israelites to separate themselves from the neighboring nations. Thus to wear hair in the style of non-Yahwistic neighbors, albeit in the context of mourning, is expressly forbidden.

Hair-cutting customs relating to mourning are thus important indicators of cultural identity, Israelite versus non-Israelite, and of various statuses within Israelite culture. While some writers demarcate clearly between nonpriestly, priestly, and high-priestly status, others appear to democratize the priesthood and proscribe hair-cutting customs in the context of mourning for all Israelites. This proscription not only reflects attitudes to the body and to holiness, but also emphasizes Israel's special status apart from other nations. What is done or not done with hair in the context of mourning creates identity and marks self-definition.

Shaving and Cleansing

Within related priestly traditions are some ritual instances in which the shaving of all body hair is prescribed. Eliminating all hair prepares priests for initiation into the priesthood and marks the healing of the leper, who after two ritual shavings can return to normal society, cleansed of his illness. Balding in cases of mourning, initiation, and healing are not unrelated. Elimination of the hair of the head or the beard suggests loss and overcoming the uncleanness of death in priestly writings pertaining to mourning, a loss which nevertheless allows for renewal. Absence of hair in the priestly initiation ceremony described in Numbers 8 and in the cleansing of the cured leper in Leviticus 14 suggest new-found wholeness. The healed person sheds the unclean status of the leper, whereas the initiation into the priesthood involves elimination of the mundane, nonsacred status of the nonpriestly person, whose cleanness still less "pure" than that required of the priest. As Olyan (1998) has emphasized, all undergo a rite of passage that allows for transformation and either reintegration into the community or assumption of a new status.

The nuance of cleansing that attaches to shaving the whole body emerges in the larger context of the initiation ritual of Leviticus 8. The hereditary Levite who is about to assume his full status and responsibilities for life is sprinkled with water of purification, just as one cleansed from the uncleanness of death is sprinkled in ritual actions described in Numbers 19. His entire body is shaved, and he washes his clothing, another common ritual of purification, which is also required after the contact with the dead (Numbers 31:19–24). A series of animal sacrifices completes the ritual pattern of initiation. The shaving of the whole body rather than merely the beard or head or a portion of these implies a complete transformation and renovation. Given that hair is equated with identity, the initiate must shed his old identity. If wholeness is holy, he manifests his transition to sacred status by being wholly shaved. Henceforth, he is not to come into contact with death and thereby contract a condition of uncleanness more unclean than the ordinary, daily, clean but mundane state. Henceforth, he is not even to shave the hair of the head or the beard in acknowledgement of mourning—not to shave in a way that shows, removing part or all of his hair. As the priestly Zadokite sumptuary rules in Ezekiel 44:20 order members of the priesthood,

> Your head you will not shave,
> and long locks *pera'* you shall not send forth.
> To trim, you shall trim your heads.

The hereditary priest is to be in a constant, reliable, seemingly unchanged state of purity and ritual readiness. He is not to wear his hair long, like Samson or the heroes of old including the priest Samuel, nor is he to shave his head, even if he mourns the loss of his father or mother. Rather, he is to wear his hair neatly trimmed, at a constant length, giving the illusion, one might assume, of always looking the same. His role is not based on charisma and serendipitous divine intervention, as in the case of Samson; rather, the priesthood and his status are hereditary. He is a priest like his father and his father before him. Nor is he to assume the appearance of an ordinary nonsacred person, subject to the unclean-rendering chaos brought about by proximity to the remains of loved ones. He is stable, and that very stability is critical to his role in society as a mediator between heaven and earth. He is always on call for such service, and his hairstyle after initiation betokens his constant status.

The person who has manifested signs of leprosy is at the opposite end of the scale from the initiated priest, having been rendered consummately unclean and having been removed from the community and his or her former position. References to hair relating to diseases of the skin have to do both with diagnosis and with the transition from a state of healing to reintegration into society. Israelite writers describe at some length so-called leprous conditions of the skin. Mary Douglas (1966) uses the term "medical materialist" for approaches that seek to explain the views of ancient writers in terms of modern notions of germs, health practices, and the like. Such an approach might suggest that the biblical priestly writers were aware of and worried about the public health implications of a contagious flesh-eating disease in their community, now identified as caused by *Mycobacterium leprae*, a particular bacillus that was very common in the ancient world. The medical materialist argument suggests that the Israelites knew to isolate those afflicted and that they developed means to distinguish between more ordinary skin infections that would heal themselves and the deadly leprosy that would consume its victim in premodern times.

A more anthropological, history-of-religions approach explains ritual practice in a nonmedical framework. To lose flesh over time is to become corpse-like, a source of the chaos of death, unclean and unwhole. Thus lepers must be separated from God's holy community. The outsider status imposed on a person who shows signs of leprosy is manifested in some of the symbols associated with the impurity of death: their clothes are to be torn, the hair on their heads disheveled. But who are lepers and who have more benign conditions that look like beginning signs of the deadly disease? Hair again plays a role. The loss of hair color, so that it appears white or yellow, is one indication of the disease (Leviticus 13:3, 21, 25, 26, 30, 32, 36). The presence of black hair, hair with pigment, is a sign of a more benign condition or of healing (see Leviticus 13:31, 37).

The leprous person who can be cleansed—that is, the person who did not have actual leprosy but a temporary skin ailment—undergoes a ritual of purification after his healing. An important part of the ritual requires the person to shave off all of his or her hair (Leviticus 14:8). He also washes his clothes and bathes. The shaving helps to effect body transformation, creating a blank slate that makes possible the return to his community. The shaving is twofold. After the first total shaving of all the hair of his body, he must stay outside his tent for seven days and then shave his body again. The Hebrew is not entirely clear. Leviticus 14:8 mentions all hair, whereas 14:9 reads "all his hair—his head, his beard, and his eyebrows, and all his hair he will shave." Does the text mean to say that the shaving includes all hair including facial and head hair (see Olyan 1998, 620) or is the second shaving less complete than the first? I tend to agree with Olyan's reading: all the hair, even the eyebrows, for example, must be shaved twice. The person thus becomes utterly smooth. His very expression is altered with the loss of eyebrows. He is in a kind of liminal phase, to use the ritual language of Victor Turner (1969), that allows the passage between his old status as an unclean leper and his new status as a cleansed person who is able to resume his normal activities and interactions. The liminal phase of rituals often involves nakedness and the removal of all signs of status, such as insignia or costume. One must become a betwixt-and-between person, having no identifiable status, in order to take up a new or renewed status. The removal of all hair of the former leper produces such a state of nakedness on the body that precedes the resumption of status. Thus, both in the ritual of priestly initiation and in the cleansing of the leper, hair is again treated as a consummate source and sign of identity and is therefore integral to the transformation or resumption of identity.

The biblical writers who describe the signs of leprosy and the possibilities for healing note that ordinary male-pattern baldness, in the absence of a rash, is no concern, but it is interesting that they feel called upon to make this point. Theirs is a culture in which hair marks normalcy and the loss of hair a potentially special or symbolically loaded situation. The writers feel the need to note that sometimes baldness is just baldness, although hairiness and smoothness can serve as significant markers of status and personality in characterizations.

Elijah, Elisha, Esau, and Jacob

Biblical tales explicitly call attention to the baldness of Elisha and to the hairiness of his master Elijah. Messengers of King Ahaziah describe the prophet Elijah, a subversive but powerful fellow who is always at odds with the Israelite aristocratic establishment, as ʾîš baʿal śēʿîr, literally "an owner or lord of hair," "a possessor of hair," "a hairy man" (2 Kings 1:8). Elijah wears a special mantle that is endowed with power and helps in the execution of miracles. Perhaps it is a garment of hair of the kind worn by the prophets alluded to in Zechariah 13:4. Elijah wears a girdle or belt of animal skin or hide. The image is of the wild. He is a man who receives divine messages from God enclosed in a mountain cave (1 Kings 19:9); he is said to be fed by ravens (1 Kings 17:4–6). The hairy prophet, who is a zealous defender of Yahwism over and against the religion of Baal, rival deity of the Canaanites patronized by members of the royal establishment, thus takes his place among heroes and charismatics, those specially loved by God. But what about his disciple, Elisha?

> Little lads came forth from the town,
> and they mocked him,
> and they said to him,
> "Go Baldy! Go Baldy!"
> He turned around, and he saw them.
> And he cursed them in the name of Yhwh,
> and come forth did two female bears,
> from the woods,
> and they ripped apart forty-two of the boys.
>
> (2 Kings 2:23–24)

This story, an Israelite version of the folk theme concerning vengeance for mocking (see Thompson 1995–1998, motif Q288), testifies to the power of the prophet. One does not mock a holy man. And it may be that the literature simply preserves a tradition of the prophet's baldness. Saint Peter is also described as bald in Christian tradition, and various apocryphal tales have been preserved about the reason for his baldness. Given how fragmentary and few are preserved written tales about particular figures, the fact that the literary tradition calls attention to the holy man's baldness may, however, be significant. Could it be that there is something incongruous about the baldness of the charismatic chosen by God? Or is the biblical writer saying that the "hairiness" is inside, not outside, and that God empowers whom he will? Elisha's punishment of the lads does seem to be an example of heavy overcompensation; two presumably very hairy she-bears swoop down upon the boys and literally split them apart. It may also be significant that the tradition makes much of Elijah's handing over his magically endowed, possibly hairy mantle to the disciple before his ascent to heaven. Does he pass on his hairiness to the bald prophet?

Another recurring visual contrast involving hair that more overtly and purposefully compares hair and the absence of hair is drawn in Genesis between the rival twin brothers Jacob and Esau. An amusing British improv group of the 1970s called "Fireside Theatre" produced a skit in which an Anglican pastor, speaking in an exaggerated parody of an upper-class Oxbridge accent, delivers a sermon on the day's reading from Genesis which begins, "My brother Esau is an hairy man and I am an smooth man." The comedians and their modern audiences no doubt found this verse from sacred scripture, taken out of context, to be incongruous and silly. What meaning can be derived from such an image? In the light of all we have discovered about hair and identity in Israelite culture, we turn to the images of Jacob and Esau's relative hairiness with appreciation and explore the significance of the contrast drawn by Israelite writers. Who might picture the men this way and why? What is the significance of the contrast for an author's identity and worldview? The ancestor hero of Israel, Jacob, father of the twelve tribes, whose name is later changed to Israel, is smooth, whereas the founding father of the neighboring, related, Semitic-speaking people, the Edomites, is hairy. What images are projected and what sort of propaganda is implicit? Why is the preserved tradition comfortable with its less hairy founding father, given the strong links we have seen in various biblical threads between hairiness, heroism, and charisma? Let us turn to Esau's hairiness in its immediate context and the wider biblical and cultural associations of the hair as contextualized.

Esau emerges first from the womb, and his hair is an immediate issue

> And emerge did the first one red,
> all of him like a mantle of hair.
>
> (Genesis 25:25)

The concept of Esau's chronological primacy is critical, as are images of "redness," the "cloak" or "mantle" and "hair." To be the firstborn within the social structure of a patrilineal society implies inheriting the father's status, lands, and clan leadership. This implicit leadership is accompanied by an appearance of ruddiness. The term for "red," *'edōm,* is related to the term for the earth, a ruddy substance. The name of the first human, Adam, a term that can be translated humanity, literally means earthling. Esau's redness is indeed related to the redness of the sandstone-rich land of the Edomites (notice the root for "redness"), descended from him in the tradition and located to the east and south of Israel. Redness thus suggests earthiness, fecundity, and humanity. It is positive for a young man to be called ruddy. The handsomeness of the young hero David is equated with being *'admônî,* ruddy (1 Samuel 16:12), the same term that describes Esau.

The cloak or mantle of hair is another loaded phrase. The prophets were known to wear hair mantles, as suggested by Zechariah 13:4. The postexilic prophet envisions a time when the prophet seeks to hide his identity because so many previous predictions have proven wrong or deceptive, a time when prophecy ceases. The absence of prophets or the prophet hiding his identity is described in terms of no longer wearing a "hairy mantle" (Zechariah 13:4). It is not known what this cloak looked like. Perhaps it was some sort of cloak made of animal skins. Elijah is "a man of hair," and his mantle appears to have special magical powers, powers passed on to the bald Elisha, who inherits his master Elijah's cloak after the master's ascent in a fiery chariot. Whether the mantle of Elijah was a hairy mantle is not explicitly stated in the text, but the associations implicit in Zechariah 13:4 are suggestive, and once again hair and the wearing of hairy clothing is positive, special. Perhaps, like the redness, the hair mantle suggests closeness to the natural end of the nature–culture continuum. The deity appears to holy men on mountains, in the wilderness. When we add to these considerations the generally positive views of abundant hair in the tales of the Hebrew Bible, especially the heroic, manly dimensions explored in chapter 3, we must conclude that, at the outset, Esau looks like a promising patriarch. This view is reinforced by the description of Jacob's birth and by the personalities and activities of the boys as they grow up.

Jacob emerges grasping the heel of his younger brother; he is second born. The older brother grows to be "a man knowledgeable in the hunt, a man of the open spaces" (Genesis 25:27). Imagery of nature, skill, and manly endeavors dominates. Jacob grows up to be what the Hebrew calls *'îš tām,* one who dwells in tents. The term *tām* comes from a root meaning "perfect" or "complete." As Koehler and Baumgartner (1994) suggest, four nuances for this root are "healthy," "well-behaved," "quiet," and "upright/honest." The New Revised Standard Version and Jewish Publication Society translations read "a quiet man." Koehler and Baumgartner (1994) also note that *tām* may mean perfect or complete in "a social sense," not rough hewn. Again, nuances of nature versus culture come to mind. They suggest translating *tām* "well-behaved," in the sense of civilized (Koehler and Baumgartner 1994, 4:1742), as does Claus Westermann (1985, 414–415). "Acculturated" or "domesticated" might be suggested. Instead of hunting, Jacob is pictured at the homestead making stew. The he-man Esau returns from the wilds hungry. Larger than life, speaking in the language of heroic exaggeration, he declares he will die without food (cf. Samson concerning dying of thirst in Judges 15:18), and the younger brother sells him stew in exchange for the elder's birthright, a deal which the elder certainly does not take seriously. The serious, grasping younger brother does.

Esau is Isaac's son. The story teller declares that the father loves him because he provides him with game to eat (Genesis 25:28). Like son, like father. He likes his food, his wild-caught food, and thinks in terms of immediate bodily rewards. He is a man of appetites, even when old and blind. Jacob, however, is his mother's favorite (Genesis 25:5). Had she not received a divine declaration that the older son would serve the younger? Jacob is "her son" (Genesis 27:6, 17), whereas Esau is Isaac's son (27:5). "Isaac loved Esau because he was food in his mouth, but Rebecca loved Jacob." It is the mother who loves her favorite boy, and it is she who masterminds the plan whereby the younger takes Esau's blessing, a significant act of trickery in a world in which blessings and curses have the power to bring about what they predict. Mother and son are both tricksters and underdogs, the woman and the second, dare we say effeminate, son, who use deception and roundabout means to further their goals. The son is ambitious; both he and his mother think of the future rather than of immediate gain; they are wily. And Jacob, the trickster, the younger, his mother's son, the domesticated man, is "a smooth man."

Rebecca discloses her plan for stealing the blessing, but Jacob worries that Isaac will recognize him and utter a curse rather than a blessing. He says, "Behold Esau my brother is a man of hair, and I am a smooth man." The word for smooth is not necessarily a complimentary one. It connotes not only the absence of hair, but also the slipperiness of the trickster. Wisdom literature warns that slippery men are not to be trusted. But Rebecca clothes him in a disguise of skins from the kid of a goat, placed on his hands and at his neck, and creates the illusion that he is Esau. The power to dress someone is an important indicator of who is in charge. The power is that of the mother furthering the career of her favorite son. The clever deception convinces the blind father, Isaac, who "does not recognize him because his hands were like the hands of Esau his brother, hairy" (Genesis 27:23). Hair is identity or assumed identity, animal-like, thick, smelling of the fields. Strong contrasts in gender and gender bending are created by the imagery of hair, and various stereotypes are at play.

The manly son is hairy, of the wild, makes manly food, and is loved by his father. The second son is smooth, soft, lives in tents, cooks, and is beloved by his mother. He and she secretly plan clever tricks together, while the father and son interact in a direct, up-front way. And yet, it is not the manly, first-born who succeeds his father in this patrilineal and patriarchal world. In the tradition, the smooth son, Jacob/Israel is father of the people Israel, and the Edomites, sons of Esau, the manly elder son, are relegated to lower status. The biblical writer seems to be rooting for Jacob, not Esau, for he describes a verbal theophany in which the deity reveals that Jacob is his choice (Genesis 25:23). Rebecca is thus portrayed to know God's plan, one which overrides human laws concerning primogeniture. What are we to conclude, then, about the voice behind these tales in Genesis and about the use of hair as it relates to worldview and culture? Why does the hairy, manly son not win? Why is Jacob portrayed as smooth?

First we must ask if one can equate body hair with the hair of the head or beard in describing the particular biblical symbol system that associates manliness with hair. It would seem that in Genesis 25–27 the relationship between manliness and hairiness is even more obvious than in tales of Samson, where a careful positional and cultural analysis allowed for a full appreciation of the gendered significance of Samson's loss of hair. Tales of Jacob and Esau do seem to partake of this gendered symbolic cluster. The fact that the smooth, more effeminate hero is the one who obtains the status and the power implies the influence of a female voice, whether produced by a woman or assumed by a man.

In her ground-breaking study of Afghan traditional tales produced primarily by one particularly talented female storyteller, Margaret Mills (1985, 1991) notes that in Afghan culture there seem to be "men's stories" and "women's stories" (1985, 187–191; 1991, 72). The stories produced by male tellers for male audiences often deal with war, heroism, and contests between men. Stories produced by women more often deal with family, marriage, and children. Both men and women produce and enjoy both varieties of stories, and some narratives contain elements of each type. One should not oversimplify, but it does seem, as one might expect, that critical subject matter concerns the particular challenges and issues faced by men or women in their daily lives. It is possible that a similar division between male and female stories is revealed in the traditional cultural media of the Hebrew Bible and that many of the tales in Genesis reflect Israelite women's stories that deal with young women's passage from father to husband, their suitors and husbands, the barrenness of the women, their childbearing woes, and the future of the children. The empowerment of smooth Jacob is thus an empowerment of women, albeit within the contours of an androcentric world. No woman warrior breaks free, no Amazon overthrows

the patriarchal system. Within that system, however, women and their surro-
gates succeed in behind-the-scenes ways through deception and trickery. The
patriarch is blind and easily fooled; the manly, hairy son follows the rules and
loses his position. The underdog in gender somehow prevails. Such stories,
portraying a loss of power to those who really hold the power in actual everyday
life, would certainly amuse women, as all such stories amuse and psychologically liberate those without power. The world of the folktale is thus liberating,
as, no doubt, are the real, private victories of women in patriarchal worlds.

Genesis 25–27, in its own way, uses the equation between hair and identity quite subversively. Even if such stories and such a use of symbols may be
rooted in women's stories and have to do with gender, something bigger is
going on; these stories are now part of the history of the people Israel, and generations of male copyists, preservers, and composers saw them as fundamental
expressions of Israelite origins and self-definition. Who was comfortable with
a smooth founding father and why?

Claus Westermann (1985) suggests that Jacob's locus in the tent and Esau's
in the wilderness reflects a paradigm shift accompanying actual socio-historical
change from early times, when people live off the land, to a later more settled
existence, with the raising of domesticated flocks (415, 417). To fully accept
Westermann's suggestion is to accept largely outdated and oversimplistic views
about the move from hunter–gatherer societies to nomadic existence to urban
life as they pertain to the history of Israel. Along his lines, however, one might
suggest that alternative paradigms of power are offered by images of Esau
and Jacob, one that valorizes brute force and simple thinking and another that
valorizes sophisticated manipulation of the system and the use of brains rather
than brawn. The latter might be expected to reflect urbane, sophisticated writers rather than country folk, although this too is probably an oversimplifica-
tion. What we can say with certainty is that the writers of the Hebrew Bible, in
various ways, love to portray the success of the disempowered who are aided
by their ever-present divine ally, the all-powerful Yhwh. God loves the weak
because their success is testimony to the realization that all power comes from
him. No one is weaker than women in the views of androcentric writers, and so
Israel becomes the female in a relationship with her protector God.

Howard Eilberg-Schwartz (1992) creatively explores the implications of Israelite men's views of themselves and their relationship with women, on the one
hand, and God on the other. Given a long history of subjugation at the hands of
ancient Near Eastern superpowers, the image of the underdog must have been
a source of great identification for Israel throughout its history, and tales of the
success of tricksters a source of satisfaction. In Genesis 25–27, absence of hair
becomes an important means of costuming the underdog appropriately. It is an

image rooted in gender and richly endowed with sociological and theological implications. Israelite writers seem to be identifying purposefully with the less hairy man, and yet that identification has meaning ironically only in a culture that values hair and sees it in contexts of male leadership, as a declaration of status and a source and symbol of power.

Joseph

Another important scene from Genesis that raises questions about absent hair has to do with the wise-man hero Joseph. Like Jacob, Joseph is a younger son. He is the favorite of his father, the son of Rachel, the favorite wife. Jacob dresses him in special garments, another important marker of status, and the older sons resent him with a vengeance. Tired of his self-aggrandizing dreams and jealous of their father's love for him, the sons eventually kidnap Joseph and sell him into slavery. Joseph is also a favorite of God and, after a series of adventures, reaches a powerful position at the Egyptian court. Joseph's prowess as a dream interpreter is made known to Pharaoh, who has had a troubling set of dreams about agricultural want and plenty—dreams of fat and lean cows and healthy and sickly ears of grain. Joseph, who languishes at this point in the palace dungeon, is brought before the king to ply his arts of dream interpretation, for no other wise man in the land can interpret the dreams. Joseph thus takes his place with Daniel, Ahiqar, and other ancient Near Eastern versions of the folktale character motif of the one person able to solve an impossible question and thereby raise or restore his status.

> And Pharaoh sent
> and he called Joseph,
> and they rushed him out of the dungeon
> and he shaved and changed his clothing,
> and he came to Pharaoh.
>
> (Genesis 41:14)

Joseph's shaving marks a change, transition, and passage. The language connotes movement. Joseph is literally made to run in a causative form of the verb (translated "rushed" above), and he comes to Pharaoh. The shaving, moreover, is linked to another important body motif of clothing. Just as his special robe had marked him as his father's favorite, one with greater status than his older brothers, the stripping of his robe by the brothers marks his loss of status. As seen in previous passages in which we discussed the relevance of Victor Turner's (1969) work on rites of passage, Joseph is the marginal or liminal figure whose transition between former and future status is symbolized by nakedness, an absence of bodily symbols. Joseph's elevation after interpreting the dream at Genesis 41:42 includes a change into elegant clothing and the donning of fine jewelry. In a similar way, here, transition is marked by a change of clothing and of hair.

In this respect, Joseph shares other traits with court figures of traditional ancient Near Eastern narrative. The emergence from a prisonlike state to freedom is often symbolized by the cutting or shaving of hair, while the state of exile, imprisonment, or immersion in chaos is symbolized by out-of-control hair. Thus in Daniel 4, King Nebuchanezzar is rendered mad by God, who punishes him for hubristically denying the power of the deity of the Israelites. He is "driven away from society" (4:22 [4:25 in English]) and becomes like an animal. "His hair grew long as eagles' [feathers] and his nails became like birds' [claws]" (4:30 [4:33 in English]). The motifs of shaggy hair and shaven hair also figure in a marvelous ancient Near Eastern tale about a wise man, Ahiqar, who has been hidden by friends after the king, under the influence of the good man's evil, power-hungry nephew, unjustly orders his execution. Ahiqar is finally rehabilitated, however, and released from a deathlike exile. He describes himself as follows: "The hair of my head had grown down on my shoulders, and my beard reached my breast, and my body was foul with the dust, and my nails were grown long like eagles'" (Ahiqar 5:11). When the king, now sorry for having ordered Ahiqar's execution, is reunited with his faithful advisor, he says, "Go to your house, Ahiqar, and shave off your hair, and wash your body, and recover your strength forty days, and after that come to me" (Ahiqar 5:13).

As Joshua Berman (2006) has noted, Joseph's actions are not merely a matter of freshening up before seeing an important person, an example of cleanliness or respect. As suggested above and as reinforced by Olyan's work on shaving customs in the Hebrew Bible, the removal of hair clearly marks transition and transformation. It is, moreover, a key motif in the plot of ancient Near Eastern court narratives. As Berman suggests, in the case of Joseph as narrated, shaving is also an important comment on matters of ethnicity and identity politics. As we have confirmed in chapter 2,

> Male Semites are routinely displayed as bearded in graphic representations in the ancient Near East, whereas Egyptians are depicted as clean shaven. One can well imagine how disconcerted Joseph must feel at the sudden and radical change to his external presentation of self, as the locks of his dark Semitic hair fall to the ground, as he runs his fingers over the face of his skin for the first time since childhood, as the guards "rush" him for his appearance before the court. (Berman 2006, 14)

Berman (2006) beautifully exercises Obeyesekere's (1981) challenge to imagine the emotions elicited by hair and the absence of hair and also perceives the change of hair in social and political terms. The beard marks Joseph's membership in a particular social group; the loss of hair marks his separation from that identity and the need to conform to that of his conquerors. He embodies a political situation whereby he must conform in order to succeed. The text is probably to be read with the active form of the verb; he shaves rather than is shaved. "He changes his clothes rather than have his clothes changed. Joseph takes preemptive action, anticipating the modes of behavior most likely to find favor with his new patron rather than waiting to be asked to conform later"(Berman 2006, 14).

Coercion is thus not physical and explicit but is implicit in the political and social setting of exile. Becoming like one's captors is a way to succeed in their world. The decision to shave or change one's hairstyle or dress or to talk differently may be undertaken with resignation or with alacrity, depending upon the situation, personality, and orientation of the marginal member of society, but this is a pattern of assimilation and accommodation seen over and over in cultures that are absorbing newcomers, whether they have arrived voluntarily or, as in the case of Joseph, involuntarily. Comparisons with issues of hair and identity in the African-American community, discussed in chapter 1, help to underscore and bring to life this scene in the tale of Joseph. The member of court who advises Pharaoh to seek Joseph's help in interpreting his dreams, in fact, refers to the foreigner as "Hebrew," a term often used in Hebrew Bible when a non-Israelite refers to an Israelite who would more likely call himself "a son of Israel." The term "Hebrew" may well be etymologically rooted in an economic socio-structural connotation rather than an ethnic one. In the ancient Near East, related terms refer to stateless, marginal folk. Thus Pharaoh's servant may be referring to the young man's social position as an outsider in Egypt. Any such slave might be "Hebrew" to the Egyptian. In any event, for Joseph to become an "insider"—and he does become the consummate insider, without whom Pharaoh makes no decision—he must shave and become like those who enslave and dominate him. It is a common theme for immigrants of all kinds and all periods. And, once again, hair is a critical marker of the acceptance, at least outwardly, of transformation from "us" to "them."

6

Letting Down Her Hair
or Cutting It Off

The Ritual Trial of a Woman Accused of Adultery
and the Transformation of the Female "Other"

The Woman Accused of Adultery

Numbers 5:11–31 describes a ritual prescribed for a married woman who is accused of adultery by her husband, in the absence of witnesses or other tangible proof. It is a particularly troubling passage for modern appropriators of biblical material, with its implications concerning men's abusive power and women's subjugation. The passage is also of special interest in the study of hair in ancient Israel, for a key symbol of the ritual involves the woman's hair and the difficult to translate term *pr'*, explored earlier in connection both with heroic hair and the uncut hair of the Nazirite vow described in Numbers 6. A first step in analysis is to listen closely to the biblical narrator, thinking in terms of Turner's (1967) exegetical and operational levels. What is done in the ritual and where does hair appear in its pattern? What nuances or attitudes are implicit in the language chosen to describe the socially disruptive situation and the supposed remedy? One can then move to a more positional and contextual analysis, asking how the hair relates to other symbols in the ritual and how the treatment of hair in Numbers 5 relates to other biblical passages concerning hair, as understood within the broader cultural framework. Important to consider is the emotional effect of the ritual on real men and women, and the ways in which the ritual involving hair reflects and affects social standing, sense of self worth, and self-definition in a particular cultural setting.

The setting for the ritual is a case when a man's wife "turns aside" and "acts against him treacherously." The text does not say explicitly that the man merely suspects his wife, but speaks in the assured declarative. She has participated in a forbidden activity. A man has lain with her, with the "laying of seed," a quite visceral description of copulation, but she has hidden it; she is "contaminated," a word used for unkosher food and forms of ritual impurity, but there is "no witness" and she has not been "found out" (Numbers 5:12–13). The reader comes to realize that the man has not caught his wife in the act or found explicit evidence; there are no witnesses. Indeed, the text states further that if a "spirit of jealousy" has come upon the man, whether she has actually become "contaminated" or not, the ritual test is prescribed.

Ritual Objects and Actions in the Context of the Passage

Central is the role of the male Levitical priest, who gathers together ritual objects, arranges them, and leads the woman through the ritual pattern. A grain offering is provided by the accusing husband: a set measure of barley grain for an "offering of jealousy," unadorned with oil or frankincense. The priest brings the woman before God at the sacred space defined by the tent or tabernacle where the divine encounters the human in rituals of mediation. He takes holy water in a clay vessel and adds dust or dirt from the earthen floor of the tabernacle. He stations the woman before God and loosens, dishevels, or lets down her hair. Specifics depend on the translation of pr˙. He places in her open hands the grain offering while he holds the water concoction called "the bitter water of the cursing." She is then to take an oath that expresses exoneration if she is guiltless and the curse of the "fallen uterus" if she is guilty. The priest writes the words of the oath on parchment and then washes them into the water; she is made to drink, literally absorbing the words. This image is evocative of a traditional world in which words have the power to bring about that which they say, an oral world in which written words and letters have a kind of special, magical power. The form of the verbs is causative: the priest causes her to take the oath and makes her drink the water (5:21, 24). Then the priest takes the offering from her hand and offers it upon the altar. If reproductive ills follow, she is deemed guilty and contaminated and bears the curse; if nothing happens, she is deemed guiltless and pure. The passage ends in noting that "the man," presumably her accusing husband, is to be considered guilt-free, no matter the results of the ritual trial. Even if his accusation turns out to be groundless, as adjudicated by the deity in this ritual action, he is not considered to have sinned, but the woman, if found to be guilty, must bear her sin.

Within this passage itself, a meaningful context for the treatment of hair emerges. First, all is in the control of men, suggesting important issues in the body politics of gender. The husband can accuse his wife in the absence of witnesses or proof, merely on the basis of "a spirit of jealousy," which may be rooted in his own insecurities, self-doubts, or animosities. He bears no guilt for making a false accusation, which may even be consciously false and undertaken to assert his power over or to take some sort of vengeance against his wife or wife's family. The male priest runs the ritual and oversees the content of the water. He offers the sacrifice, he alters her hair, he makes her drink, he states the curse, and he has her make the oath. The treatment of the hair, then, is part of this process of men's taking and exhibiting control of the woman. A part of her body, her hair, is loosed, in some way undone by the priest in response to the husband's accusation. This involuntary altering of hair is an intrusive act of intimacy and an assertion of power, as seen in cases of absent hair and the shaving of Samson's hair. Here men have power over women's hair. This invasion of her body space subjugates the woman and enhances the empowerment of the men around her. The ritual provides an excellent example of the way in which a private symbol becomes public statement: she is accused, vulnerable, and can be exonerated only though this invasion of her body. Thus she is silenced and demeaned, no matter what the outcome of the ritual. The threat of such a ritual might indeed be a means of control that a husband could hold over his wife. The hair, let down, also relates to the symbols of water, earth, clay, and barley grain within the passage.

Presumably, before the priest's action, the hair was not "loose" or "let free" or "disheveled," but was set in some culturally recognized fashion. I discuss this social context and its implications below, looking back at artistic representations and at some instructive biblical passages. But even taking the passage alone, it is clear that all of the above symbols are in some way natural, unadorned, as they are: an unfired earthen pot, dust taken from an unfinished earthen floor, basic unrefined grain without enhancements of the texture or aroma, and water. Thus the loose hair is naked hair, natural hair. All of these symbols point to exposure of the crime or innocence; the truth is made open. The seedy grain, the water, and the earth also suggest fertility, the materials necessary to grow vegetation. It is the depositing of inappropriate seed in the improper place that worries the husband, that is, the use of his wife's womb by a man other than himself. The freed hair in the context of these symbols may also suggest, then, her sexuality and her fertility, which is let loose and unpacked to be examined by men. Hair does not always connote sexuality in some universal fashion, but the sexual nuance seems plausible in this gendered setting where the central issue is the woman's sexual availability, and where hair is accompanied by symbols of seed, earth, and water.

Context in Culture: Positional Analysis and Cultural Body

In moving beyond the passage itself, with its cluster of symbols, its nuances of language, and its operational description of what is done, we first turn to non-verbal representations of Israelite women's hair. As in the case of the Nazirite vow of Numbers 6, to best understand what it means to alter hair, one needs to know how it might have been worn before the alteration. Art may provide some information. As discussed in chapter 2, Assyrian reliefs of the eighth century BCE that depict the defeat of the Judean city Lachish and the exile of its people include portrayals of adult women. The Assyrian artists depict the women with heads covered by a clothlike headgear or shawl that descends the length of the body. The hair is not seen. Perhaps it is chin-length or longer beneath the covering, or held back with pins. The purpose of the head covering may be modesty or protection from the sun and dust during the journey. Once again, one must rely on the representations by the conquerors, which may or may not be accurate. Another direction of inquiry may be provided by the pillar figurines, which suggest a variety of elaborate and simpler hairstyles, some with the hair reaching to the shoulders or neck and others to the chin.

A few biblical passages also provide some hints concerning women's hairstyles. One of the liveliest metaphoric descriptions in the Bible, in Song of Songs 4:1, imagines the long beautiful hair of a young woman.

> Behold, you are beautiful, my darling.
> Behold, you are beautiful.
> Your eyes are doves,
> from behind your veil.
> Your hair is like a flock of goats
> that leap down from Mt. Gilead.

Some suggest that the poet pictures waves of dark tresses falling about the woman's shoulders or breasts. The image of leaping (or reclining) goats seems to emphasize thickness, curliness, quantities of hair, a mass of tresses. The companion in the Song is a young woman of an age before marriage. She is pictured, in various speeches, to express her longing for a handsome young lover, the shepherd, whether real or imagined. He is her first love. Her speeches alternate with those of the young man, who describes the beauty of the young woman's various features using a host of metaphors. Whether young women in an Israelite setting would have worn their hair long and free or whether this imagery is the fantasy of the poet, assuming the role of the shepherd lover, we cannot know. Did young, unmarried women customarily wear their hair down, as in many cultures, or does the image reflect the writer's male erotic fantasy? The context is quite different from that of Numbers 5, although here. too. the male voice is pictured to control or create the woman's hair, albeit in a benevolently sensuous way.

A fascinating passage in Isaiah 3:24 may reveal something about the typical hairstyle of adult women of an aristocratic class. The eighth-century BCE prophet chastises the "daughters of Zion," employing the misogynistic motif of the wayward woman to capture and express the sinfulness of the people of Judah. Isaiah insists they have broken covenant with God and that they will be punished in war by the superpower Assyria. After describing the daughters as virtual harlots decked out in flashy, expensive clothing and jewelry, he states that all their finery will be taken away. Isaiah's message is theological to be sure, but it also has to do with class and with gender. The sins of the people as described in Isaiah 1 involve oppression of the poor by those in power. Isaiah 3:14–15 makes it clear that the prophet's condemnation is directed against those who have the power to oppress: the rich, those in leadership (elders, princes of his people). He believes, moreover, that the social world has become a chaos in which women control the men (see 3:12: "women rule over them"). The women whose hairstyle is described are thus clearly pictured as aristocrats; that he chooses a feminine image not only has to do with a stock motif in the prophetic repertoire whereby the unfaithful people Israel is compared to an unfaithful wife (e.g., Hosea 2, Jeremiah 2, Ezekiel 16), but perhaps also with his own resentment of some aristocratic women's political power.

> Instead of perfume, rot there will be,
> and instead of a sash, a captive's rope.
> Instead of well-set hair, baldness,
> and instead of a rich robe, a girding of sackcloth.

The phrase translated "well-set hair" is rooted in the word "to do," literally "a deed or matter," and in the adjective meaning "stiff" or "hard." A related word refers to the artistic metalwork of the tabernacle. That the phrase does indeed refer to hair in Isaiah is made clear by the "baldness" with which it is contrasted. As in the image of the perfume that becomes stinking rot, so another feature of a woman's toilette turns from beauty to ugliness. An image of living luxuriously turns into a reminder of death; a cameo of cultural order turns to chaos. The woman's hair normally, then, is set artistically and with care. Dayagi-Mendels (1993) reads this passage to suggest a style with "hair gathered and rolled into a knot at the back of the head, or a rolled up plait held by a pin in the Mesopotamian style" (76, 77).

It is not certain whether we can assume that the young Israelite woman, the *bĕtûlāh*, wore her lair loose and long as in the Song of Songs and that the married, well-to-do woman wore her hair pulled back in some way, but it is a possibility. What, then, does the term *pr'* mean in the context of Numbers 5? We would assume that the well-set hair is let down, disheveled, freed, and appears longer than it would before this action by the priest takes place, all of which are visual possibilities within the range of the term's meanings in the Hebrew Bible. Just as in the Nazirite vow, the term *pr'* must reflect hair that normally appears shorter, less obvious than before the vow or the action.

The symbol of grain as it appears in the offering of jealousy also connotes a special natural status compared with other typical grain offerings in the Bible. In Leviticus 21:1 and 6:7, 14–15, the flour is of a finer quality and is treated with oil and frankincense to make a richer, aromatic offering to the deity (see also Leviticus 2:13). The very simple quality of the offering of "jealousy," by comparison, suggests a stripping bare, a return to basics, and thus goes well with the symbol of the hair which is not beautified, tied, pinned, or set.

The positional analysis of the ritual scene described in Numbers 5 also invites comparison with two other types of ritual and or legal action in the biblical tradition. One involves the case in which a possible crime has been committed but, as in Numbers 5, no witnesses have come forth and guilt or innocence hangs in doubt. The other specifically involves women, several cases in which the expected social patterns of patrilineal culture have been interrupted by the husband's death, by the wife's infidelity, or by a daughter's rape. Both sorts of material have to do with a necessary passage from doubt, uncertainty, or social dislocation to clarity, resolution, and return to a social status quo.

Deuteronomy 21:1–9 describes a situation in which a corpse has been found, suggesting the victim's murder, but the perpetrator of the crime cannot be ascertained. Such a situation of doubt must have been particularly destructive in small communities where everyone knew everyone else. Whether a local person is suspected or a passing stranger is believed to have been the perpetrator, the uncertainty is destructive and unsettling. This ritual provides a means whereby leaders of the community virtually or symbolically reenact the crime with an animal victim, take corporate responsibility, and then cleanse themselves of guilt.

The ritual for the woman suspected of adultery can be seen in a similar context marking a passage from socially destructive uncertainty to clarity. In this context, nothing can be hidden. The hair is made symbolically free in a public setting. As in the rites of passage described by Turner (1969), there are three phases: the situation and status before the ritual action, the betwixt-and-between phase when the ritual passenger makes transition, and the final phase when structure is reasserted or a new status is established. The in-between phase is often marked by the removal of signs of status, such as clothing or insignia, or by nakedness. The loosed hair marks such a liminal or transitional phase. Hair done up a certain way probably signifies the woman's status as an adult, married woman; hair neatly arranged signifies normality, whereas disheveled hair signifies rupture and uncertainty. After the ritual, the woman will either be reintegrated into society or cast out. Either way, from a social perspective, the fissure is healed. Gender issues regarding place in social structure, certainty, and the discomfort of social uncertainty also come into play.

In ancient Israelite culture, women's ideal socio-structural roles move along expected life patterns. A young woman is a virgin in her father's household and under his control. Her sexuality is his to bestow upon a future husband via exchange arrangements, sometimes involving varieties of dowry and bride price. Then she becomes a faithful, child-producing wife in her husband's household. Events or situations that interfere with these ideal configurations challenge the social structure and are dealt with through ritual, custom, or legal machination. The virgin who is raped, whereby her sexuality is breached without her father's permission, the barren wife, the unfaithful wife, and the childless widow are all marginal figures, threats to the status quo according to important threads in Israelite culture. Thus in the Hebrew Bible means are suggested to repair the social structure, and these solutions are presented from an androcentric point of view. The feelings or wishes of the woman do not generally appear to be taken into account. Neatening up the social structure can regularize her position in some cases or even protect her physically and economically, but this makes sense within the dominant culture in which the critical relationships are those that bind men.

Thus the virgin who is raped can be married off to the rapist by her father. Her position is thereby regularized, although such a solution strikes the modern reader as utterly callous. It is always difficult to identify with aspects of alien cultures. Is rape always rape? Can it be seduction? Can it be a matter of not getting a father's permission? Notice the language of Deuteronomy 22:28 and Exodus 22:15 (verse 16 in English): seduction in the latter passage, probably ravishing in the former. The least one can say is that all such situations are lumped into one category regarding the solution: regularizing her position from the men's perspective either by marrying her off or by having the rapist pay the father for loss of her womb's worth.

The unfaithful wife can be stoned, thereby eliminating the problem and assuring that male lineages remain intact and unconfused by another lineage's seed (Deuteronomy 22:22–24). The childless widow may be married off to her deceased husband's brother in order to raise up children in the husband's name (Deuteronomy 25:5). His line thereby continues, as does her connection to the patrilineage that she joined in marriage. As in the case of the raped woman, marrying off the childless widow provides her with context and stability in a patriarchal world that has few safety nets for those rendered marginal by the system. Paradoxically, the same can be said for women accused by rabidly jealous husbands of committing adultery.

The accusation of adultery in the absence of evidence or witnesses is a socially disruptive act. As in the case of the unsolvable murder, a small community might spin out of control with suspicion, accusation, and individual acts of vengeance. The trial by "the water of bitterness," conducted by the mediating priest, resolves these tensions in a ritual fashion that has the deity be the adjudicator, and his decision is final. The ritual allows for the erasure of uncertainty and either for the required rehabilitation of the woman or for her being cast out. In the hands of a skilled priest, the situation of a chronically jealous, irrational husband could be dealt with successfully. Community pressure and fear of God would require him to continue to support her as his wife and would at least temporarily quiet him. To be sure, this is not the sort of marriage counseling offered by modern family therapists and in no way takes into account the abusive nature of the relationship between the husband and the wife. The primary interests, again, are in the maintenance of male lineages and in the return to some sort of status quo that is not disruptive of the social fabric. In this gendered context, the letting down of the woman's hair not only marks a passage from disruption to the restoration of social order in an androcentric world, but also clearly marks power relations. The woman's hair is rearranged by the priest; her fate, her person, is in his hands. The hair becomes a metonym for her status and identity. By the same token, should she be found innocent, she can resume her marriage, rehabilitated and renewed. Naked hair also betokens a fresh start, a return to beginnings. Psychoanalytically, such a fresh start seems problematical. The bitter emotions and feelings of betrayal would no doubt make it extremely difficult simply to start over.

Nevertheless, this is the goal of ritual passage, to cleanse, make a fresh slate, and recommence.

The Captive Bride

Equally multilayered and thought provoking regarding matters of gender, cultural identity, and transformation is Deuteronomy 21:10–14, another passage pertaining to women's hair. The setting for this text is war; the writer describes ritual patterns that mark the entry and exit from battle (see Deuteronomy 20:1–20). Deuteronomy 21:10–14 describes the prescribed treatment of one of the most valuable and vulnerable spoils of war, captured women. The subject of the case is described as "a good-looking" or beautiful woman among the captives of war. One of the Israelite conquerors, addressed in the second person in the passage, is said to "love her" or to become "attached to her," and takes her for a wife. It is interesting first, that the word used for "wife," which literally means "woman," is not the term for second wife, concubine, or slave. It is the usual term for any wife, whereas other terms were available that would more fully suggest lower status in the marriage. And later, the language at 21:13 speaks of "marrying her." The full translation of verse 13 is interesting in what it reveals about the androcentrism of the Hebrew and the culture it reflects and shapes: You (the man) may go into her (a phrase with sexual connotations, implying consummation or betrothal through intercourse), marry her (a term rooted in the word "master" so that the husband is "master" and "to marry" is "to become master over the woman"), and she will be to you a wife (literally "woman" as above). The language suggests that any wife is had sexually, that her husband masters her, and that she becomes his woman. Nuances of ownership are implicit. Sexist as it is, the language is not ethnocentric and does not draw a distinction between this wife and other Israelite wives. The language reflects the usual terminology for any marriage, and the captive wife is treated like any woman, however ambiguous that status.

The captive's beauty might be seen as capital that sets her apart from other women of the defeated enemy camp and allows for her to be regularized socially and economically. Less beautiful women might become slaves. Of course, one might well ask whether the woman would appreciate this regularization or regard it as forced marriage and rape, an arrangement made for the benefit of the conquering power without the appropriate address to father, kin, and custom. Issues concerning point of view—male versus female, conqueror versus conquered—frame these troubling ambiguities and set the stage for the treatment of the captive woman's hair.

The returned soldier is to bring the beautiful woman to his household. The process of transfer from one status and identity to another begins. There,

> she will shave her head
> and pare her nails,
> and remove her captive's garment
> and she will stay in your house,
> and mourn [literally cry over] her father and mother,
> for a month's days.
>
> (Deuteronomy 21:12–13)

The term for "shave" is a common one used in a variety of events concerning the intentional loss of hair, whether intended by the shaver or the one who is shaved. This term is used in connection with the leper in the process of purification (Leviticus 14:8); in instructions for the Nazir whose status is interrupted by contact with the dead or who finishes the vow period and returns to mundane status (Numbers 6:9, 18; see also 2 Samuel 14:26 on Absalom and implicit nuances concerning his cut hair); as a symbol of defeat (Isaiah 7:20); and as a form of unmanning and asserting control (Samson: Judges 16:17; the emissaries of David: 2 Samuel 10:4). As noted by Saul Olyan (1998), all of these instances of shaving connote a process of transformation. Within the context of the passage, shaving the head joins other symbols of change: the cutting of nails, which like the hair are part of the person, curiously growing and yet capable of being severed without pain; the change of clothing; seclusion, the time apart from social intercourse; the status of mourning whereby dear ones have been lost and one faces life without them. As in the case of the woman accused of adultery, the loss of hair, like the letting down or disruption of the set, socially marked hairstyle, marks the liminal phase in a rite of passage. Old identity has been shed in order for new identity to be asserted. The young woman is being unmade in order to be remade. Shaving the hair alters the woman even more radically than the letting down or loosening of hair. The shaved hair, together with cutting of the nails and removal of clothing, are powerful symbols of the transformation of the social body. Hair and clothing especially mark social and cultural identity, as evidenced by the various artistic representations of conquered peoples by ancient Near Eastern artists. From the perspective of the Israelites, the woman is being made "not them" and potentially "one of us."

Issues of purification are also at play in this passage preserved in the priestly corpus of Numbers. For these writers the captured "Other" is a source of contagion and uncleanness. Numbers 31:16–20 makes a case for the necessity of cleansing all captured spoil, animate and inanimate. Indeed, all male captives, child or adult, and all mature women who have had sex with men are to be eliminated lest they contaminate the holy people. This harsh ideology of war, so at odds with modern theories of just war, partakes of the rigidly intolerant ideology of the "ban as God's justice," whereby the death of the enemy is justified and, in fact, required. Such people are regarded as sources of uncleanness and temptation that might lure Israel to worship gods other than Yhwh (see Numbers 31:16; Deuteronomy 7:1–6; Niditch 1993, 56–89). Numbers 31, however, makes an exemption for virgin girls—they have not been with a man and they are not future warriors. Such girls are clean slates, not yet marked by the identity of the male Other.

Permanent and indelible cultural and ethnic identity is thus understood as male. Women are here imagined as gardens for men's seed and become fully identified as belonging to an ethnic group after belonging to a man and being "marked," in a sense, by a man of that group. In Deuteronomy 21, it is not overtly stated that the woman is a virgin girl, and perhaps any woman is meant, which would allow more possibility for transformation of the woman even after sexual contact with the male alien Other. However, note that she mourns not for husband or children left behind but precisely for her parents, identifying her, probably, as a younger, unattached woman in line with Numbers 31. Even so, she must be made anew; she who belonged to them culturally must be emptied of an old identity to assume a new one. In contrast to those who undertake transformation through shaving voluntarily (e. g., the voluntary Nazir who knows that at a certain time the vow will be complete and the hair will be shaved), the woman has shaving imposed upon her. The perspective of the writers of this material dominates.

The verbs describing the captive woman's actions are in the imperfect tense, which can simply connote future action, but here the connotation seems to be one of enforcement, what she has to do, is willed to do. It is possible that the writer imagines the woman to share a set of symbols and customs with the Israelites and that the rites of transformation are intercultural signs of mourning over family and people lost to her; she herself may be imagined to want to undertake these signs of transformation. Balding, in particular, connotes mourning. She is in mourning over the fate of her family and over her own fate. But she clearly has no choice but to be transformed. Such is the destiny of captured women in the cruel Mediterranean world, reflected also in the many descriptions of the fate of the Trojan women in classical Greek literature. The rules of body politics, controlled by the male winners of battle, require her loss of hair, as the rules of male spouses and priestly leaders require and control the accused woman's alteration of hair.

The treatment of the captured woman, when viewed from exegetical, personal, and emotional perspectives, reveals some interesting discomfort on the part of those in control. The text states that if the woman does not please her

husband after marriage, he can terminate the relationship. This is unfortunately the prerogative of any Israelite husband, although community pressure,
as discussed for the woman accused of adultery but found to be innocent, may
have some mitigating influence on those who would summarily or capriciously
divorce their wives. In any event, should this man dismiss the foreign wife,
he cannot now treat her as a slave and sell her. He must let her go free, for he
has "humiliated" her. The word used for his taking her as wife is a form of the
verbal root that means "to be bowed down, afflicted." This form of the verb is
specifically used to mean "rape" in Genesis 34:2; Deuteronomy 21:14; 22:24, 29;
Judges 19:24; 20:5; and 2 Samuel 13:12. This verb describes both the way Sarah
treats Hagar and the way the Egyptians treat the Israelites in slavery. In other
words, this term specifically refers to a man's improperly helping himself to a
woman's sexuality against proper social sanction as well as to other forms of
oppression. To describe what the man has done to the captured woman with
this term questions the ethical propriety of his actions as conqueror and is an
overt admission on the part of the controlling voice of the passage that all is not
right in this way of obtaining a wife.

For the woman who is shaved, one can only imagine the emotional dimensions of her experience. With the shaving of her hair, she is receiving a concrete
sign of her domestication, submission, and loss of her previous life. It is doubt-
ful that awareness of shaving as a feature of transformation rituals especially
related to mourning necessarily provided the same type of comfort as when
undertaken in one's own society with the support of members of one's own culture. The woman might reach a point of resignation in the need to survive, but
transformation for her would not be a process of renewal. For her, loss of her
hair is deeply about loss of identity, loss of self, and loss of cultural context.

These two passages about women's hair in the control of men send messages about the personal body, the social body, the body politic, and the perme-
ability of identity that underscore the vulnerability of women in the ancient
world. We are all subject to the forces of chaos in the form of disease, war, and
death. Women's status is even more ambiguous in that men can manipulate
that status to shore up their own sense of security, control, ownership, and
orderliness. This control is illusory, to be sure, for chaos has power over us all,
but one way men convey and reinforce their illusion is by their capacity to alter
women's hair.

7

Conclusions

This study of hair in ancient Israel has been informed by a rich collection of comparative ethnographic materials and by awareness that each culture is unique, multifaceted, complex, dynamic, and subject to change. The contributions of anthropologists, sociologists, art historians, and scholars of religion have framed the work.

An important model throughout has been Victor Turner's (1969) version of Arnold van Gennep's (1960/1908) astute observations about rites of passages, those recurring ritual patterns by which cultural groups and their members mark and achieve changes in status. The growing, cutting, shaving, or other alteration of hair relates, as Saul Olyan (1998) has discussed with reference to Israelite culture, to alterations in status. Intentionally created baldness, in particular, suggests the middle or liminal phase in a transformation when the "passenger" has shed one identity and not yet assumed or renewed another. Such passages, which feature the alteration of hair, overtly or implicitly suggest ritual patterns and processes, whether they relate to mourning customs, healing rituals, immersion into holiness, the return to mundane status, humiliation and conquest, or the life stages of a hero. In all cases, some sort of refashioning takes place, and hair symbolism relates integrally to other sorts of symbols to create complex webs of meaning and message as culturally expressed. Hair, whether grown long, shaved, or intricately arranged, is related to larger threads of cultural meaning and tradition concerning various sorts of status—ethnic identity, gender, degree of holiness—all potentially overlapping forms of self-definition.

To uncover some of these meanings, anthropologists like Turner actually interview participants in a cultural tradition, observe ritual actions, and live in the setting. Students of ancient cultures are limited to remains. Physical evidence is partial and sometimes damaged, separated from its full living context; written materials are edited and represent a mere fraction of the various verbal traditions, oral and written, which once reflected and shaped cultures. The full context and meaning of extant literature and implicit alternative points of view are difficult to reconstruct. Nevertheless, one can adapt Turner's (1967) categories of exegetical, operational, and positional analysis to attempt to hear the ancient writers and artisans as if they were native informants. Context is critical throughout; the context of references to hair within a particular narrative or description and the wider biblical context and tradition to which images of and attitudes to hair belong.

Turner's (1967) exegetical level of analysis suggests concern with the ways in which individuals set in cultural contexts relate to or understand their hair, headgear, or changes in hairstyle. The works of Gananth Obeyesekere (1981, 1990, 1998) and Scheper-Hughes and Lock (1987) encourage the exegete to seek out the emotional, personal, and psychological roots, dimensions, and responses of Israelites who, for example, might have assumed the temporary Nazirite status described in Numbers 6. Attention to the personal leads the reader to try to understand the underlying characterization of Absalom as a man who takes pleasure in displaying his beautiful thick hair, but whose hair is then his undoing. This approach challenges us to think about the way a woman accused of adultery by her husband might feel at having her hair let down. We are moved to think about the emotional effect of having one's hair shaved for a hero like Samson, whose hair has grown since birth, or about the response of the foreign captive woman, separated from home and family, to having her head shaved. One might ask further about the way a visiting Judean dignitary to the court of Sennacherib might feel upon seeing his countrymen portrayed as the defeated enemy in the Lachish reliefs, for he would recognize his fellows, both men and women, in part by their headgear.

An important question throughout is whether the hair/head treatment is culturally condoned, expected, and participatory or imposed on the individual. Is it a voluntary or involuntary condition? Samson's long hair is culturally situated, a possible marker of the special son of a barren woman, and yet it is involuntary, a status determined before his birth. The shaving of his hair is imposed upon him, although the psychologically complex tale suggests it was not unexpected. The shaving of the heads of David's emissaries is not condoned but involuntary and carries various implications about shame and honor in men's cultures. Joseph voluntarily makes his face look smooth like that of his overlords and adopts a hairstyle to fit in and further his career, but such alterations of hair, as Joshua Berman (2006) notes, are undertaken with ambivalence and are not really completely voluntary. The voices of various African-American women concerning hair and cultural identity, explored in chapter 1, suggest interesting parallels and a similar kind of dissonance. The categories of "social body" and "body politic," as explored by Scheper-Hughes and Lock and their various scholarly antecedents, are relevant in this context of voluntary and involuntary hairstyles. Hairstyles and customs reflect and affect shared cultures as well as developments and variations within those cultural traditions, but they are also a means by which one group or power can impose itself on those in its grasp.

A study of portrayals of hair in ancient Near Eastern art introduces the integral relationship between hair and ethnic identity. I discussed some of the ways in which producers of the art represented "our" heads and hair versus "theirs" and the significance of these contrasts. To some extent, dominant powers can control through artistic representations the identity of those they subjugate, especially for future generations of viewers. Egyptian, Assyrian, or Persian in origin, the paintings and reliefs are products of their own artistic culture, with its ideological orientation, presuppositions, conventions, and techniques. Several scholars point out that while such portrayals may identify enemy peoples as defeated and subjugated, they can also show them bearing an ethnically distinctive hairstyle as part of the rich cultural diversity of the empire, a part of a positive whole. Obeyesekere's (1981, 1990) work urges us to think, for example, about the complex and conflicted responses to these images on the part of Israelite visitors to Sennacherib's court (emissaries, tribute bearers, royalty) who might have seen themselves portrayed in Assyrian art. How might those who actually fought at Lachish have reacted to representations of themselves and their comrades, their fleeing wives, children, and neighbors? Would such portrayals have reinforced their own sense of ethnic identity or robbed them of it?

The portrayals of the hairstyles and headgear of Philistines, Israelites, Egyptians, Canaanites, and Syrians in ancient Egyptian art do perhaps reflect actual ethnic, aesthetic, and cultural differences that shed light both on Egyptian views of others and upon biblical motifs and messages about hair. Philistines, portrayed at Medinet Habu as smooth shaven and possibly with hair invisible under stiff hats, and Israelites, possibly portrayed at Karnak with beards and long hair held back by a fillet, help create visual images as one imagines Israelites warriors confronting Philistines in the epic tales of the Hebrew Bible. Samson, the especially long-haired charismatic Nazir, who has grown his locks over the course of a life-time, thus makes for a stunning ethnographic contrast with his enemies the Philistines. Indeed, tales of Samson are quintessentially about us versus them—about cultural, political, and ethnic conflict.

Pictorial evidence of smooth-shaven Egyptians allows one to understand better the significance of Joseph shaving before his audience with Pharaoh. The shorter hair of eighth-century BCE male Judeans, portrayed in the Lachish reliefs of Sennacherib's palace, may indicate a change in hairstyle and taste from Egyptian portrayals of Bronze Age warriors, although one cannot be certain about developments in hairstyle (the evidence is too meager), about the influence of local artistic conventions in such portrayals, or even if the men with short, curly hair are Egyptians or Nubians rather than Judeans. If Israelite or Judean men did generally wear their hair shorter during the eighth century than in the twelfth century BCE, in a kind of cropped style, it might explain why a Nazirite vow not to cut the hair for a specified time would be noticeable in this later period. Women are portrayed with heads covered at Lachish, so we cannot easily speculate about their demeanor as voluntary Nazirites. Would women under such a vow be expected to allow their hair to be seen in public and thereby signal their holy status, or was this aspect of the vow expected to be kept private, so that not partaking of wine or participating in funerals would be the more obvious markers of the temporary holy status for women? Were some women's hairstyles chin length as in some of the Judean female figurines, so that, as in the case of the men, hair left uncut for a time would be noticeable?

The contrast between Samson's variety of Nazirism and that of Numbers 6 is perhaps one of the most interesting ways in which tracing attitudes toward hair allows one to trace threads in Israelite literature, social history, and thought and to learn about the special orientation and self-interests of the priestly source of Numbers 6. The Nazirism of Samson is related to the description of warriors in Judges 5:2, Deuteronomy 32:42, the Nazirism of Samuel, the hairiness of Elijah, the poetic description of Amos 2:10–11, and the pretensions of Absalom, pretender to his father David's throne. These examples suggest an association between long hair, warrior status, manliness, charisma, and holiness. Absalom is not a Nazir, but his long, thick hair beautifully allows the author ironically to depict both his desire for status and power and precisely those very traits of leadership he lacks. Charismatic Nazirism involves divine selection—from birth in the cases of Samuel and Samson—permanent status, and the avoidance of wine products and unclean food. Charismatic Nazirism is nonvoluntary in that God selects the hero for his own reasons or the mother regards him as a special gift which she gives back in service to the deity. The status often involves participation in war and always requires being male. Nazirism in Numbers 6 is voluntary, expands the prohibition of grape products, and emphasizes the avoidance of corpses with a particular priestly orientation concerning maintenance of ritual purity. The status is available to men and women. It does not involve war and is noncharismatic. The voluntary Nazir might well temporarily remake himself or herself in the ancient, Nazirite image to project some of those leadership qualities implied by the hair in long-standing traditions. It is also likely that charismatic Nazirites still arose in Israel in postmonarchic times, but that the priestly passage in Numbers 6 attempted to democratize the status and make it available to all Israelites. There are a number of religious and political reasons for the writers' interest in this shift of the Nazirite paradigm.

The shapers of the priestly traditions of Numbers anticipate later Rabbinic thinking in their efforts to expand and more fully apply certain aspects of priestly orientation to the lives of non-Levitical members of the community. It is interesting, for example, as noted above, that the prohibition against wine consumption, mentioned in the tale of Samson, is more fully elaborated in Numbers (see Numbers 6:3). The treatment of death as a source of uncleanness is also expanded in Numbers.

Samson's need to avoid the dead is not mentioned in Judges 13 (see 13:4–5, 7, 14 and compare to Numbers 6:3–4), and even in Leviticus, another work shaped by priestly writers, corpses do not seem to be the source of contagion they are held to be in Numbers 19. Only priests in Leviticus need worry about the contaminating results of contact with bodies of the dead, whereas Numbers 19 makes corpses contaminating for all Israelites and prescribes rituals of cleansing. The authors of Numbers democratize a supreme source of uncleanness and thereby suggest that all Israelites are holy on some level, not only priests who offer sacrifices in the sacred space. One sees a similar extension of holiness in Numbers 6, with an additional requirement for the Nazir. For him or her, as for all Israelites in Numbers 19, contact with the chaos of death renders one unclean, but during the Nazir's voluntary assumption of temporary holiness, he is not to allow himself, if he can possibly avoid it, to become unclean through contact with the dead; even the corpses of close relatives are to be avoided. The ordinary Israelite is acknowledged to become unclean when someone near to him or her dies, and is then ritually cleansed in accordance with the ritual described in Numbers 19; the Nazir, however, like the priest, must try to avoid ever becoming unclean during the period of his or her vow. The priestly proscription against contact with the dead applies to the Nazir.

On the one hand, one is tempted to suggest that the priestly writers of Numbers are opening up matters in their purview to ordinary Israelites. All are rendered unclean by contact with the dead, and some individuals, are, if possible, to avoid the dead altogether so that their holiness remains intact during the period of the vow. On the other hand, this very process of democratization, while it seems like a means of sharing of holiness, is actually a means by which priests retain more power and control. The priests responsible for the description in Numbers 6 have attempted to co-opt and domesticate Nazirism, safely bounding that explosive, divinely ordained, charismatic sort of holiness that may descend upon any son of a barren woman or any superhero. Such holy men may be threats to the establishment, to the powers that be, and the priests responsible for Numbers imagine themselves as central, establishment authorities who rule with God's will and the approval of the Persian court.

Thus, in Numbers, priests control the ritual passages of the Nazir and determine if the vow has been interrupted by contact with the dead. Priests' holiness, moreover, is permanent and hereditary, whereas the holiness of voluntary Nazirites is temporary. Finally, one might argue that, in this androcentric world, allowing women to assume Nazirite status truly puts the phenomenon in its place as a lesser sort of holiness than that of the male priests, albeit a means for women to reach what may be for them a meaningful degree of religious expression. The sacrificial offerings required and the activities that need to be avoided may suggest that Nazirism was appealing and available to the wealthy, and I have discussed who such men and women might have been in a Persian period setting. The emphasis on personal piety seems appropriate to a postexilic world in the light of other biblical genres and motifs of this period. Thus this important custom relating to hair contrasts the traditional model of the Nazir with a priestly innovation and thereby sheds some light on the political, economic, and religious dynamics at play in the Persian period. The possibility that the voluntary Nazir may be male or female also raises fundamental issues in gender that have formed an important thread throughout our study.

Building on images of Samson and other charismatic Nazirites, I have explored the ways in which loss of hair is related to concepts of masculinity. Control of hair and hairstyle implies male and female roles, metaphorically or literally. When David's emissaries are shaved by Ammonite enemies (1 Samuel 10:4–5), their responses and that of the king who sent them imply they have been humiliated and unmanned. Together with the symbolic tearing of the bottom of their garments, the imagery suggests feminization and invokes within Israelite warrior culture emotions of deep shame and humiliation. Thus Isaiah describes defeat by Assyria as Israel's having its "head, pubic hair, and beard" swept away by the enemy king, imaged as a "razor" (Isaiah 7:20). Such scenes are, as Emily Vermeule (1979) has discussed, the stock-in-trade of epic warrior accounts in which the defeated enemy is the one who is had, raped, and made the woman by the victorious warrior. This sort of imagery, inviting to interpretations influenced by Freud (1950/1922) and Foucault (1980), informs Jael's assassination of the Canaanite general Sisera in Judges 4:21 and 5:27. In this case, with additional irony, the woman becomes the warrior who turns the man into a woman. In 2 Samuel 10 and Isaiah 7, however, the imagery is invoked not by scenes of battle or assassination but by the symbolism of shaved hair.

The imagery becomes more complicated when it is the national hero, Jacob, who is born to be smoother than his older brother, who is deemd to be inferior by the Israelite writers. The younger, smooth Jacob, the one loved by his mother, a mama's boy, inherits the mantle of leadership, and Esau, the older, hairy, manly, hunter son, beloved by his father, is tricked out of his birthright and his blessing. I explored the implications of this play between hairy and smooth for Israelite identity and the paradoxical identification with the feminine in a consummately androcentric culture. Questions concerning the woman's voice in literary material and the imagery of the underdog and the trickster come into play.

Finally, I explored less ambivalently gendered ritual patterns involving women and hair, the treatment of the woman captive, and the ritual trial of the woman accused of adultery by her husband in the absence of witnesses. Both of these passages subjugate women in disturbing ways through the imagery of hair, shaved in the first instance and let down in the second. The role of the priest is paramount in Numbers 5, as in other material preserved by priestly writers. In a world controlled by men, at least in the overt legal sense, the water trial might actually be employed to rehabilitate the woman, but this seeming liberation from false accusation binds her to the continuation of a form of everyday imprisonment. The jealous husband suffers no punishment for accusing her again and again. Hair that is loosened suggests openness, nakedness, and the natural state, a means to ascertain the truth but also a means of exposing the accused woman. Similarly, the captive foreign woman is made anew, purified by the loss of her hair, and, while the participants in these ancient Near Eastern cultures may have accepted this treatment with some resignation, the point of view in Deuteronomy 21 is that of the captors, Israelite men, interested in new wombs in which to plant Israelite seed and in altering the woman so that she becomes "us" and not "them." The very language of oppression in this passage, however, suggests guilt on the part of the captors. With the loss of her hair, cutting of her nails, and change of her clothing she is objectified and humiliated, even while being transformed.

The study of hair in ancient Israel provides an entry into the rich literary traditions of this culture and its dynamic, varied, and sometimes competing ideologies. Israelites, like all human beings set in culture, wear their worldviews and weave their culture in images and customs of hair. The study of hair reveals attitudes toward gender, ethnicity, holiness, beauty, leadership, and economic status. Hair and head treatments reflect and shape both cultural and personal identity; actual hairstyles and portrayals of hair in verbal and nonverbal art contribute to the process of self-definition and are integral to the way we are and how others view us. In the study of hair in ancient Israel, I have tried to further our understanding of actual hair customs and practices in Israelite and neighboring cultures and to explore the various symbolic roles of hair and transformations of hair, its emotional and evocative effect on wearers and viewers, its cultural messages and meanings, and its political power and influence.

References

Albenda, Pauline. 1982. "Egyptians in Assyrian Art." *Bulletin of the Egyptological Seminar* 4: 5–23.

Aldred, Cyril. 1980. *Egyptian Art in the Days of the Pharaohs 3100–320 B.C.* New York: Oxford University Press.

Alter, Robert. 1990. "Samson without Folklore." In *Text and Tradition: The Hebrew Bible and Folklore*, ed. Susan Niditch. Atlanta: Scholars Press. Pp. 47–56.

Arthur, Linda B, ed. 1999. *Religion, Dress and the Body.* Oxford: Berg.

Avigad, N. 1987. "The Contribution of Hebrew Seals to an Understanding of Israelite Religion and Sociey." In *Ancient Israelite Religion*, eds. Patrick D. Miller, Paul D. Hanson, and S. Dean McBride. Philadelphia: Fortress Press. Pp. 195–208.

Bal, M. 1884. "The Rhetoric of Subjectivity." *Poetics Today* 5:337–376.

Banks, Ingrid. 2000. *Hair Matters: Beauty, Power, and Black Women's Consciousness.* New York: New York University Press.

Barkay, Gabriel. 2006. "Royal Palace, Royal Portrait? The Tantalizing Possibilities of Ramat Raḥel." *Biblical Archaeology Review* 32: 34–44.

Barnett, Richard David. 1958. "The Siege of Lachish." *Israel Exploration Journal* 8: 161–164.

———. 1960. *The Assyrian Palace Reliefs and Their Influence on the Sculptures of Babylonia and Persia.* London: Batchworth.

———. 1976. *Sculptures from the North Palace of Ashurbanipal at Nineveh (668–627 B.C.).* London: British Museum Publications.

———. 1982. *Ancient Ivories in the Middle East.* Qedem 14. Monographs of the Institute of Archaeology Hebrew University of Jerusalem. Jerusalem: Institute of Archaeology.

————, Erica Bleibtrau, and Geoffrey Turner. 1998. *Sculptures from the Southwest Palace of Sennacherib at Nineveh.* 2 Vols. London: British Museum Press.

Batulukisi, Niangi. 2000. "Hair in African Art and Culture." In *Hair in African Art and Culture,* eds. Roy Sieber and Frank Herreman. New York: Museum for African Art. Pp. 25–37.

Becher, Jeanne, ed. 1991. *Women, Religion and Sexuality: Studies on the Impact of Religious Teachings on Women.* Philadelphia: Trinity Press International.

Beck, Pirhiya. 1982. "The Drawings from Horvat Teiman (Kuntillet ʿAjrud)." *Tel Aviv* 9: 3–68.

Bendix, Regina, and Dorothy Noyes, eds. 1998. "In Modern Dress: Costuming the European Social Body, 17th–20th Centuries." Special Issue. *Journal of American Folklore* 111.

Berg, Charles. 1951. *The Unconscious Significance of Hair.* London: George Allen and Unwin.

Berger, John. 1977. *Ways of Seeing.* London: Penguin.

Berman, Joshua. 2006. "Identity Politics in the Burial of Jacob (Genesis 50:1–14)." *Catholic Biblical Quarterly* 68 : 11–31.

Berquist, Jon L. 2006. "Constructions of Identity in Post-Colonial Yehud." In *Judah and Judeans in the Persian Period,* eds. Oded Lipschits and Manfred Oeming. Winona Lake, IN: Eisenbrauns. Pp. 53–66.

Bloch-Smith, Elizabeth. 2003. "Israelite Ethnicity in Iron I: Archaeology Preserves What Is Remembered and What Is Forgotten in Israel's History." *Journal of Biblical Literature* 122: 401–425.

Boling, Robert. 1975. *Judges: Introduction, Translation, and Commentary.* AB 6A. Garden City, NY: Doubleday.

Bordo, Susan. 1993. *Unbearable Weight: Feminism, Western Culture and the Body.* Berkeley: University of California.

————. 1999. *The Male Body: A New Look at Men in Public and in Private.* New York: Farrar, Straus and Giroux.

Bourdieu, Pierre. 1984. *Distinction: A Social Critique of the Judgement of Taste.* Trans. R. Nice. Cambridge, MA: Harvard University Press.

Boyarin, Daniel. 1993. *Carnal Israel: Reading Sex in Talmudic Culture.* Berkeley: University of California.

Breitbart, Eric. 1997. *A World on Display. Photographs from the St. Louis Fair World's Fair 1904.* Albuquerque: University of New Mexico Press.

Brown, F., S. R. Driver, and C. A. Briggs. 1968. *A Hebrew and English Lexicon of the Old Testament.* Oxford: Oxford University Press.

Brown, Peter. 1971. "The Rise and Function of the Holy Man in Late Antiqity." *Journal of Roman Studies* 61: 80–101.

Bynum, Caroline Walker. 1987. *Holy Feast and Holy Fast: The Religious Significance of Food to Medieval Women.* Berkeley: University of California Press.

Carter, Charles Edward. 1992. "A Social and Demographic Study of Post-Exilic Judah." PhD diss., Duke University.

Chapman, Cynthia R. 2004. *The Gendered Language of the Warfare in the Israelite-Assyrian Encounter.* Harvard Semitic Monographs 62. Winona Lake, IN: Eisenbrauns.

Cheng, Weikun. 1998. "Politics of the Queue: Agitation and Resistance in the Beginning and End of Qing China." In *Hair: Its Power and Meaning in Asian Cultures,* eds. Alf Hiltebeitel and Barbara D. Miller. Albany, NY: SUNY Press. Pp. 123–142.

Cifarelli, Megan. 1998. "Gesture and Alterity in the Art of Ashurnasirpal II of Assyria." *The Art Bulletin* 80: 210–228.

Coakley, Sarah. 1997. *Religion and the Body.* Cambridge: Cambridge University Press.

Collon, Dominique. 2005. "Examples of Ethnic Diversity on Assyrian Reliefs." In *Ethnicity in Ancient Mesopotamia.* Papers Read at the 48th Rencontre Assyriologique Internationale, Leiden, July 1–4, 2002, ed. W. H. Van Soldt. Leiden: Nederlands Instituut voor het Nabije Oosten. Pp. 66–77.

Coogan, Michael D. 1998. "In the Beginning. The Earliest History." In *The Oxford History of the Biblical World,* ed. Michael D. Coogan. New York: Oxford University Press. Pp. 3–31.

———. 1978. "A Structural and Literary Analysis of the Song of Deborah." *Catholic Biblical Quarterly* 40:146–166.

Cooper, W. 1971. *Hair: Sex, Society, Symbolism.* New York: Stein and Day.

Craigie, P. C. 1968. "A Note on Judges V2." *Vetus Testamentum* 18: 397–399.

Dayagi-Mendels, Michal. 1993. *Perfumes and Cosmetics in the Ancient World.* Jerusalem: Israel Museum.

Delaney, Carol. 1995. "Untangling the Meanaings of Hair in Turkish Society." In *Off with Her Head: The Denial of Women's Identity in Myth, Religion, and Culture,* eds. Howard Eilberg-Schwartz and Wendy Doniger. Berkeley: University of California Press. Pp. 53–75.

Dever, William G. 1984. "Asherah, Consort of Tahweh? New Evidence from Kuntillet 'Ajrud." *Bulletin of the American Schools of Oriental Research* 255: 21–37.

Douglas, Mary. 1966. *Purity and Danger: An Analysis of Concepts of Pollution and Taboo.* New York: Praeger.

Eilberg-Schwartz, Howard, ed. 1992. *People of the Body: Jews and Judaism from an Embodied Perspective.* Albany, NY: SUNY Press.

Eilberg-Schwartz, Howard, and Wendy Doniger, eds. 1995. *Off with Her Head: The Denial of Women's Identity in Myth, Religion, and Culture.* Berkeley: University of California Press.

Finkelstein, Israel. 1985. "Response." In *Biblical Archaeology Today: Proceedings of the International Congress on Biblical Archaeology: Jerusalem, April 1984,* ed. A. Biran. Jerusalem: Israel Exploration Society. Pp. 80–83.

Firth, Raymond. 1973. "Hair as Private Asset and Public Symbol." In *Symbols: Public and Private.* Ithaca, NY: Cornell University Press. Pp. 262–298.

Foley, John Miles. 1991. *Immanent Art: From Structure to Meaning in Traditional Oral Epic.* Bloomington: Indiana University Press.

Foucault, Michel. 1980. *The History of Sexuality.* Vol. 1, *An Introduction.* Trans. Robert Hurley. New York: Vintage Press.

Franklin, N. 1994. "The Room V Reliefs at Dur-Sharruken and Sargon II's Western Campaigns." *Tel Aviv* 21: 255–275.

Freud, Sigmund. 1950/1922. "Medusa's Head." In *Collected Papers*, vol. 5, ed. James Strachey. London: Hogarth Press. Pp. 105–106.

Galpaz-Feller, P. 2004. "Hair in the Hebrew Bible and in Ancient Egyptian Culture: Cultural and Private Connotations." *Biblische Notizen* 125: 75–94.

Gatens, Moira. 1996. *Imaginary Bodies: Ethics, Power, and Corporeality*. New York: Routledge.

Gennep, Arnold van. 1960/1908. *The Rites of Passage*. Chicago: University of Chicago Press.

Geva, Shulamit. 1981. "The Painted Sherd of Ramat Raḥel." *Israel Exploration Journal* 31: 186–189.

Gordon, Cyrus H. 1965. *Ugaritic Textbook*. Rome: Pontifical Biblical Institue.

Grosz, Elizabeth. 1994. *Volatile Bodies: Toward a Corporeal Feminism*. Bloomington: Indiana University Press.

Hackett, Jo Ann. 1998. "'There Was No King in Israel': The Era of the Judges." In *The Oxford History of the Biblical World*, ed. Michael D. Coogan. New York: Oxford University Press. Pp. 177–218.

Hadley, Judith M. 2000. *The Cult of Asherah and Ancient Israel and Judah*. Cambridge: Cambridge University Press.

Hall, H.R. 1928. *Babylonian and Assyrian Sculpture in the British Museum*. Paris: Les Éditions G. Van Oest.

Hallpike, C.R. 1969. "Social Hair." *Man* 4: 256–264.

Haynes, J. L. 1977–1978. "The Development of Women's Hairstyles in Dynasty Eighteen." *Journal of the Society for the Study of Egyptian Antiquities* 8: 18–24.

Hero. 2002. Dir. Zhang Yimou. DVD. Buena Vista.

Herreman, Frank. 2000. "Hair: Sculptural Modes of Representation." In *Hair in African Art and Culture*, eds. Roy Sieber and Frank Herreman. New York: Museum for African Art. Pp. 47–57.

Hershman, P. 1974. "Hair, Sex and Dirt." *Man* 9:274–298.

Hiltebeitel, Alf. 1998a. "Introduction: Tropes." In *Hair: Its Power and Meaning in Asian Cultures*, eds. Alf Hiltebeitel and Barbara D. Miller. Albany, NY: SUNY Press. Pp. 1–9.

———. 1998b. "Hair Like Snakes and Mustached Brides: Crossed Gender in an Indian Folk Cult." In *Hair: Its Power and Meaning in Asian Cultures*, eds. Alf Hiltebeitel and Barbara D. Miller. Albany, NY: SUNY Press. Pp. 143–176.

Hiltebeitel, Alf, and Barbara D. Miller, eds. 1998. *Hair: Its Power and Meaning in Asian Cultures*. Albany, NY: SUNY Press.

Hobsbawm, Eric. 1981. *Bandits*. New York: Pantheon Press.

Hogland, Kenneth G. 1992. *Achaemenid Imperial Administration in Syria-Palestine and the Misssions of Ezra and Nehemiah*. SBLDS 125. Atlanta, GA: Scholars Press.

Holladay, John S., Jr. 1987. "Religion in Israel and Judah under the Monarchy: An Explicitly Archaeological Approach." In *Ancient Israelite Religion: Essays in Honor of Frank Moore Cross*, eds. Patrick D. Miller, Paul D. Hanson, and S. Dean McBride. Philadelphia: Fortess. Pp.249–99.

Holladay, William L. 1986. *Jeremiah 1: A Commentary on the Book of the Prophet Jeremiah, Chapters 1–25*. Philadelphia: Fortress Press.

Hollywood, Amy. 1999. "Transcending Bodies." *Religious Studies Review* 25:13–18.

Jacoby, R. 1991. "The Representation and Identification of Cities on Assyrian Reliefs." *Israel Exploration Journal* 41: 112–31.

Janzen, J. Gerald. 1989. "The Root *pr`* in Judges V 2 and Deuteronomy XXXII 42." *Vetus Testamentum* 39: 393–406.

Jastrow, Marcus. 1950. *Dictionary of the Targumim, the Talmud Babli, the Yerushalmi, and the Midrashic Literature*. New York: Pardes Publishing House.

Jastrow, Morris, Jr. 1914. "The 'Nazir' Legislation." *Journal of Biblical Literature* 44: 266–285.

Kadish, Gerald E. 2001. "Karnak." In *Oxford Encyclopedia of Ancient Egypt,* vol. 2, ed. Donald Redford. Oxford: Oxford University Press. Pp. 222–226.

Keel, Othmar, and Christoph Uehlinger. 1998. *Gods, Goddesses and Images of God in Ancient Israel*. Trans. Thomas H. Trapp. Minneapolis, MN: Fortress Press.

Killebrew, Ann E. 2005. *Biblical Peoples and Ethnicity. An Archaeological Study of Egyptians, Canaanites, Philistines, and Early Israel*. Atlanta, GA: Society of Biblical Literature.

King, L.W. 1915. *Bronze Reliefs from the Gates of Shalmaneser*. London: The British Museum.

King, Philip J., and Lawrence E. Stager. 2001. *Life in Biblical Israel*. Louisville: Westminster/ John Knox.

Kitchen, Kenneth. 2004. "The Victories of Merenptah and the Nature of their Record." *Journal for the Study of the Old Testament* 28: 259–272.

Kletter, Raz. 1996. *The Judean Pillar-Figurines and the Archaeology of Asherah*. Biblical Archaeology Review International Series 636. Oxford: Tempus Reparatum.

Knoppers, Gary N. 2006. "Revisiting the Samarian Question in the Persian Period." In *Judah and the Judeans in the Persian Period,* eds. Oded Lipschits and Manfred Oeming. Winona Lake, IN: Eisenbrauns. Pp. 265–289.

Koehler, Ludwig, and Walter Baumgartner. 1994. *The Hebrew and Aramaic Lexicon of the Old Testament* (subsequently revised by Walter Baumgartner and Johann Jakob Stamm). Leiden, the Netherlands: Brill.

Laud, Gordon. 1939. *The Megiddo Ivories*. Chicago: University of Chicago Press.

Law, Jane Marie, ed. 1995. *Religious Reflections on the Human Body*. Bloomington: Indiana University Press.

Lawal, Babatunde. 2000. "Orilonise: The Hermeneutics of the Head and Hairstyles among the Yoruba." In *Hair in African Art and Culture,* eds. Roy Sieber and Frank Herreman. New York: Museum for African Art. Pp. 93–109.

Leach, Edmond R. 1967. "Magical Hair." In *Myth and Cosmos. Readings in Mythology and Symbolism,* ed. John Middleton. Garden City, NY: Natural History Press. Pp. 77–108.

Levine, Molly Mayerowitz. 1996. "The Gendered Grammar of Ancient Mediterranean Hair." In *Off with Her Head: The Denial of Women's Identity in Myth, Religion, and Culture,* eds. Howard Eilberg-Schwartz and Wendy Doniger. Berkeley: University of California Press. Pp. 76–130.

Lévi-Strauss. Claude. 1983. *The Raw and the Cooked*. Trans. John and Doreen Weightman. Chicago: University of Chicago Press.

Lincoln, Bruce. 1977. "Treatment of Hair and Fingernails among the Indo-Europeans." *History of Religions* 16: 351–362.

Lucas, A. 1930. "Ancient Egyptian Wigs." *Annales du Service des antiquités de l'Égypte* 30: 190–196.

Luft, Ulrich H. "Religion." In *Oxford Encyclopedia of Ancient Egypt*, vol. 3, ed. Donald Redford. Oxford: Oxford University Press. Pp. 139–145.

Machinist, Peter. 2000. "Biblical Traditions: The Philistines and Israelite History." In *The Sea Peoples and Their World: A Reassessment*, ed. Eliezer D. Oren. Philadelphia: The University Museum. Pp. 53–83.

Mageo, J. 1994. "Hairdos and Don'ts: Hair Symbolism and Sexual History in Samoa." *Man* 29: 407–432.

Mallowan, M. E. L. 1966. *Nimrud and Its Remains*. London: Collins.

Mauss, Marcel. 1973. "Techniques of the Body." *Economy and Society* 2(1): 70–88.

Mazar, Amihai. 1992. *Archaeology of the Land of Israel*. New York: Doubleday.

McCarter, P. Kyle. 1980. *1 Samuel: A New Translation with Introduction, Notes, and Commentary*. Anchor Bible 8. Garden City, NY: Doubleday.

———. 1987. "Aspects of the Religion of the Israelite Monarchy: Biblical and Epigraphic Data." In *Ancient Israelite Religion: Essays in Honor of Frank Moore Cross*, eds. P.D. Miller et al. Philadelphia: Fortress Press. Pp. 137–155.

Meyers, Carol. 1997. "The Family in Early Israel." In *Families in Ancient Israel*, eds. Leo G. Perdue, Joseph Blenkinsopp, John J. Collins, and Carol Meyers. Louisville, KY: Westminster/John Knox Press. Pp. 1–47.

Miles, Margaret. 1985. *Image as Insight: Visual Understanding in Western Christianity and Secular Culture*. Boston: Beacon Press.

Miller, Barbara. 1998. "Afterword: Hair Power." In *Hair: Its Power and Meaning in Asian Cultures*, eds. Alf Hiltebeitel and Barbara D. Miller. Albany, NY: SUNY Press. Pp. 281–286.

Mills, Margaret A. 1985. "Sex Role Reversals, Sex Changes, and Transvestite Disguise in the Oral Tradition of a Conservative Muslim Community in Afghanistan." In *Women's Folklore, Women's Culture*, ed. Rosan A. Jordan and Susan J. Kalčik. Philadelphia: University of Pennsylvania Press. 187–213.

———. 1991. "Gender and Verbal Performance Style in Afghanistan." In *Gender, Genre, and Power in South Asian Expressive Traditions*, eds. Arjun Appadurai, Frank J. Korom, and Margaret A. Mills. Philadelphia: University of Pennsylvania Press. Pp. 56–77.

Mobley, Gregory. 1997. "The Wild Man in the Bible and the Ancient Near East." *Journal of Biblical Literature* 116:217–233.

Moorey, P.R.S. 1988. "The Peoples of the Empire." In *The Cambridge Ancient History*. Plates to vol. 4. Cambridge: Cambridge University Press. Pp. 40–44.

———. 1994. *Ancient Mesopotamian Materials and Industries. The Archaeological Evidence*. Oxford: Clarendon Press.

Morrow, Wille. 1973. *400 Years without a Comb*. San Diego: Black Publishers.

Müller, Maya. "Relief Sculpture." In *Oxford Encyclopedia of Ancient Egypt*, vol. 3, ed. Donald Redford. Oxford: Oxford University Press. Pp. 133–139.

Mumcuoglu, Yani K., and Joseph Zias. 1988. "Head Lice: *Pediculus humanus capitis* (Anoplura Pediculidae) from Hair Combs Excavated in Israel and Dated from the First Century B.C. to the Eighth Century A.D." *Journal of Medical Entomology* 25: 545–547.

Naguib, Saphinaz-Amal. 1990. "Hair in Ancient Egypt." *Acta Orientalia* 51: 7–26.

Narkiss, Bezalel. 1985. "Introduction." In *Ancient Jewish Art*, ed. Gabrielle Sed-Rajna. Neuchâtel, Switzerland: Imprimerie Paul Attinger. Pp. 9–29.

Naveh, Joseph, and Shaul Shaked. 1985. *Amulets and Magic Bowls: Aramaic Incantations of Late Antiquity*. Jerusalem: Magnes Press.

Niditch, Susan. 1989. "Eroticism and Death in the Tale of Jael." In *Gender and Difference in Ancient Israel*, ed. Peggy L. Day. Minneapolis, MN: Fortress Press. Pp. 43–57.

———. 1990. "Samson as Culture Hero, Trickster, and Bandit: The Empowerment of the Weak." *Catholic Biblical Quarterly* 52: 608–24.

———. 1993. *War in the Hebrew Bible: A Study in the Ethics of Violence*. Oxford: Oxford University Press.

———. 1996. *Oral World and Written Word: Ancient Israelite Literature*. Louisville, KY: Westminister/John Knox.

Noth, Martin. 1968. *Numbers: A Commentary*. Trans. James D. Martin. Old Testament Library. London: SCM Press.

Obeyesekere, Gananath. 1981. *Medusa's Hair: An Essay on Personal Symbols and Religious Experience*. Chicago: University of Chicago Press.

———. 1990. *The Work of Culture: Symbolic Transformation in Psychoanalysis and Anthropology*. Chicago: University of Chicago Press.

———. 1998 "Foreword." In *Hair: Its Power and Meaning in Asian Cultures*, eds. Alf Hiltebeitel and Barbara D. Miller. Albany, NY: SUNY Press. Pp. xi–xvi.

O'Connor, David. 2000. "The Sea Peoples and the Egyptian Sources." In *The Sea Peoples and Their World: A Reassessment*, ed. Eliezer D. Oren. Philadelphia: University of Pennsylvania Press. Pp. 85–102.

Olivelle, Patrick. 1998. "Hair and Society: Social Significance of Hair in South Asian Traditions." In *Hair: Its Power and Meaning in Asian Cultures*, eds. Alf Hiltebeitel and Barbara D. Miller. Albany, NY: SUNY Press Pp. 11–49.

Olyan, Saul M. 1998. "What Do Shaving Rites Accomplish and What Do They Signal in Biblical Ritual Contexts?" *Journal of Biblical Literature* 117: 611–622.

———. 2005. "Some Neglected Aspects of Israelite Internment Ideology." *Journal of Biblical Literature* 124: 601–616.

Porter, Barbara Nevling. 2003. *Trees, Kings, and Politics. Studies in Assyrian Iconography*. Orbis Biblicus et Orientalis 197. Freibourg, Germany: Academic Press/Vandenhoeck & Ruprecht.

Pritchard, James B. 1969. *The Ancient Near East in Pictures*. Princeton, NJ: Princeton University Press.

Rabin, Chaim. 1955 "Judges 5:2 and the 'Ideology' of Deborah's War." *Journal of Jewish Studies* 6:125–34.

Reade, Julian. 1999. *Assyrian Sculpture*. Cambridge, MA: Harvard University Press.

Redford, Donald B. 1992. *Egypt, Canaan and Israel in Ancient Times*. Princeton, NJ: Princeton University Press.

―――. 2000. "Egypt and Western Asia in the Late New Kingdom: An Overview." In *The Sea Peoples and Their World: A Reassessment*, ed. Eliezer D. Oren. Philadelphia: University of Pennsylvania Press. Pp. 1–20.

―――, ed. 2001. *The Oxford Encyclopedia of Ancient Egypt*. New York: Oxford University Press.

Redmount, Carol A. 1998. "Bitter Lives: Israel in and out of Egypt." In *The Oxford History of the Biblical World*, ed. Michael D. Coogan. New York: Oxford University Press. Pp. 79–121.

Roberts, J.J.M. 2006. "Isaiah's Egyptian and Nubian Oracles." In *Israel's Prophets and Israel's Past: Essays on the Relationship of Prophetic Texts and Israelite History in Honor of John H. Hayes*, eds. Brad E. Kelle and Megan Bishop Moore. Library of Hebrew Bible/Old Testament Studies 446. New York/London: T & T Clark. Pp. 201–209.

Robins, Gay. 1994. *Proportion and Style in Ancient Egyptian Art*. Austin: University of Texas Press.

―――. 1997. *The Art of Ancient Egypt*. Cambridge, MA: Harvard University.

―――. 1999. "Hair and the Construction of Identity in Ancient Egypt." *Journal of the American Research Center in Egypt* 36: 55–69.

Rooks, Noliwe M. 1996. *Hair Raising: Beauty, Culture, and African American Women*. New Brunswick, NJ: Rutgers University Press.

Rushing, Andrea Benton. 1988. "Hair-Raising." *Feminist Studies* 14: 325–335.

Russell, John Malcolm. 1991. *Sennacherib's Palace without Rival at Nineveh*. Chicago: University of Chicago Press.

―――. 1993. "Sennacherib's Lachish Narratives." In *Narrative and Event in Ancient Art*, ed. Peter J. Holliday. Cambridge: Cambridge University Press. Pp. 55–73.

―――. 1998. *The Final Sack of Nineveh: The Discovery, Documentation, and Destruction of Sennacherib's Throne Room at Nineveh, Iraq*. New Haven, CT: Yale University Press.

Russmann, Edna R. 2001. "Aspects of Egyptian Art." In *Eternal Egypt. Masterworks of Ancient Art from the British Museum*. Berkeley: University of California Press. Pp. 28–45.

Scheper-Hughes, Nancy and Margaret Lock. 1987. "The Mindful Body: A Prolegomenon to Future Work in Medical Anthropology." *Medical Anthropology Quarterly* 1: 6–41.

Shaughnessy, Dan. Oct. 5, 2003. "Sox Try to Change Luck in Battle to Stay Alive." *Boston Globe*. Pp. A-1, C-4.

Seow, Leong. 2007. "The Social World of Ecclesiastes." In *Scribes, Sages, and Seers: The Sage in the Eastern Mediterranean World*, ed. Leo Perdue. Göttingen, Germany: Vandenhoeck & Ruprecht, forthcoming.

Shulman, David D. 1986. "Battle as Metaphor in Tamil Folk and Classical Traditions." In *Another Harmony*, eds. Stuart M. Blackburn and A. K. Ramanujan. Berkeley: University of California Press. Pp. 105–130.

Sieber, Roy. 2000a. "Prologue and History." In *Hair in African Art and Culture*, eds. Roy Sieber and Frank Herreman. New York: Museum for African Art. Pp. 15–23.

————. 2000b. "A Note on Hair and Mourning Especially in Ghana." In *Hair in African Art and Culture*, eds. Roy Sieber and Frank Herreman. New York: Museum for African Art. Pp. 89–91.

————, and Frank Herreman, eds. 2000. *Hair in African Art and Culture*. New York: Museum for African Art.

Siegman, William. 2000. "Women's Hair and Sowei Masks in Southern Sierra Leone and Western Liberia." In *Hair in African Art and Culture*, eds. Roy Sieber and Frank Herreman. New York: Museum for African Art. Pp. 71–77.

Smith, Morton. 1987. *Palestinian Parties and Politics That Shaped the Old Testament*. London: SCM Press.

Smith, W. Stevenson. 1998. *The Art and Architecture of Ancient Egypt*, 3rd ed. Revised by William Kelly Simpson. New Haven: Yale University Press.

Soggin, J. Alberto. 1981. *Judges: A Commentary*. Trans. Jolin Bowden. OTL. London: Westminster Press.

Stager, Lawrence E. 1985a. "Merenptah: Israel and Sea Peoples. New Light on an Old Relief." *Eretz-Israel* 18: 56–64.

————. 1985b. "The Archaeology of the Family in Ancient Israel." *Bulletin of the American School of Oriental Research* 260: 1–35.

————. 1998. "Forging an Identity: The Emergence of Ancient Israel." In *The Oxford History of the Biblical World*, ed. Michael D. Coogan. New York: Oxford University Press. Pp. 123–175.

Synnott, A. 1993. *The Body Social: Symbolism, Self, and Society*. London: Routledge.

Temin, Christine. Sept 29, 2002. "Hair Today. Contemporary Artists Go to Great Lengths to Explore Its Power and Meanings." *Boston Globe*. Pp. N-1, N-8.

Thomas, Christine. 2006. "Samson Went down to Timnah: Ethnicity, Kinship and Sexual Relations in Judges 14." Paper presented at the Annual Meeting of the Society of Biblical Literature, Washington, DC, November 17–21.

Thompson, Julia J. 1998. "Cuts and Culture in Kathmandu." In *Hair: Its Power and Meaning in Asian Cultures*, eds. Alf Hiltebeitel and Barbara D. Miller. Albany, NY: SUNY Press. Pp. 219–258.

Thompson, Stith. 1955–1958. *The Motif Index of Folk Literature*. Bloomington: Indiana University Press.

Turner, Victor. 1967. "Themes in the Symbolism of Ndembu Hunting Ritual." In *Myth and Cosmos: Readings in Mythology and Symbolism*, ed. John Middleton. Garden City, NY: The Natural History Press. Pp. 249–269.

————. 1969. *The Ritual Process*. Ithaca, NY: Cornell University Press.

Uberoi, J.B. Singh. 1967. "On Being Unshorn." *Transactions of the Indian Institute of Advanced Study* 4: 87–100.

Uehlinger, Christoph. 2003. "Clio in a World of Pictures—Another Look at the Lachish Reliefs from Sennacherib's Southwest Palace at Nineveh." In *'Like a Bird in a Cage': The Invasion of Sennacherib in 701 BCE*, ed. Lester L. Grabbe. Journal for the Study of the Old Testament Supplement 363. Sheffield: Sheffield, Academic Press. Pp. 221–305.

Ussishkin, David. 1982. *The Conquest of Lachish by Sennacherib*. Tel Aviv: Tel Aviv University.

Vaughan, James A. 2000. "Hair Style among the Margi." In *Hair in African Art and Culture*, eds. Roy Sieber and Frank Herreman. New York: Museum for African Art. Pp. 111–115.

Vermeule, Emily. 1979. *Aspects of Death in Early Greek Art and Poetry*. Berkeley: University of California Press.

Wachsmann, Shelley. 2000. "To the Sea of the Philistines." In *The Sea Peoples and Their World: A Reassessment*, ed. Eliezer D. Oren. Philadelphia: University of Pennsylvania Press. Pp. 108–143.

Wäfler, Markus. 1975. *Nicht-Assyrer neuassyrischer Darstellungen: Alter Orient und Altes Testament 26*. Neukirchen-Vluyn: Neukirchen Verlag.

Watson, James L. 1998. "Living Ghosts: Long-Haired Destitutes in Colonial Hong Kong." In *Hair: Its Power and Meaning in Asian Cultures*, eds. Alf Hiltebeitel and Barbara D. Miller. Albany, NY: SUNY Press. Pp. 177–193.

Weitzman, Steven. 2002. "The Samson Story as Border Fiction." *Biblical Interpretation* 10: 158–74.

Westermann, Claus. 1985. *Genesis 12–36: A Commentary*. Trans. John J. Scullion. Minneapolis, MN: Augsburg Publishing House.

Wilson, Robert R. 1980. *Prophecy and Society in Ancient Israel*. Philadelphia: Fortress Press.

Winter, Irene J. 1981. "Royal Rhetoric and the Development of Historical Narrative in Neo-Assyrian Reliefs." *Visual Communication* 7/2: 2–38.

———. 1997. "Art in Empire: The Royal Image and the Visual Dimensions of Assyrian Ideology." In *Assyria 1995*, Proceedings of the 10th Anniversary Symposium of the Neo-Assyrian Text Corpus Project, Helsinki, September 7–11, 1995, eds. S. Parpola and R. M. Whiting. Winona Lake, IN: Eisenbrauns. Pp. 359–381.

Yoder, Christine Roy. 2003. "The Woman of Substance (אשת־חיל): A Socioeconomic Reading of Proverbs 31:10–31." *Journal of Biblical Literature* 122: 427–447.

Young, Katharine, and Barbara Babcock, eds. 1994. "Bodylore." *Journal of American Folklore* 107.

Yurco, Frank. 1990. "3,200-Year-Old Pictures of Israelites Found in Egypt." *Biblical Archaeology Review* 16:20–38.

———. 1997. "Merenptah's Canaanite Campaign and Israel's Origins." In *Exodus: The Egyptian Evidence*, eds. Ernest S. Frerichs and Leonard H. Lesko. Winona Lake, IN: Eisenbrauns. Pp. 27–55.

General Index

Biblical Index